Break Ground

On Learning How to Pray

Margaret M. Calkin

Copyright © 2002 by Margaret M. Calkin

Break Ground
by Margaret M. Calkin

Printed in the United States of America

Library of Congress Control Number: 2002103452
ISBN 1-591600-51-0

All rights reserved. No part of this publication may be reproduced or transmitted in any form or by any means without written permission of the publisher.

Scripture references marked KJV are from the King James Version of the Bible.

Scripture taken from the HOLY BIBLE INTERNATIONAL VERSION OF THE BIBLE © 1946, 1952, 1971 by Division of Christian Education, National Council of the Churches of Christ in the USA.

Scripture references marked RSV are from the REVISED STANDARD VERSION OF THE BIBLE © 1946, 1952, 1971, Division of Christian Education, National Council of the Churches of Christ in the USA.

Scripture references marked NRSV are from the NEW REVISED STANDARD VERSION OF THE BIBLE © 1989, Division of Christian Education, National Council of the Churches of Christ in the USA.

Scripture references marked TLB are from *The Living Bible* © 1971 by Tyndale House Publishers, Wheaton, IL. All rights reserved.

All scripture taken from THE AMPLIFIED BIBLE, Old Testament © 1965, 1987 by the Zondervan Corporation. THE AMPLIFIED NEW TESTAMENT © 1965, 1987, by the Lockerman Foundation. Used by permission..

Xulon Press
11350 Random Hills Road
Suite 800
Fairfax, VA 22030
(703) 279-6511
XulonPress.com

To order additional books, call 1-866-909-BOOK (2665).

Introduction

The second time I was born I discovered that I was starving and terribly thirsty. I'm sure that is true of most newborns, especially the babes in Christ who have just received Jesus as Lord and Savior. My soul was saved, but it sure needed food and drink, the kind that can only come from the Holy Spirit. The path to nurture lay in prayer. Simply put, I had to learn to pray if I was going to abide with the Lord and dine with him.

As I stumbled and scrambled down the long road of spiritual growth, I often wished I could find a simple text written in conversational style about the process of learning to pray. I yearned for some very simple down-to-earth instruction on achieving heavenly communication. I wanted a beginner's manual.

Years later, I remembered that desire when I received the inspiration for writing this small book as a reference and resource for Christians wishing to learn more about prayer. Within these pages, I offer the lessons I have absorbed through study and personal experience. Since I have written from an ecumenical perspective, I encourage you to take what you want and to leave the rest in the hands of the Lord. He alone knows how to speak to your heart. I am only a helper to the Teacher of Prayer.

The Master was faithful and kind to give special support to

me during my season of writing. Loving Christians with the skill sets I needed just popped into my life in God's perfect timing. People came to offer spiritual counseling, advice, editing, criticism, and computer skills. I cannot even remember all of those who have contributed to this effort. However, God knows each and every one, and I pray that he will bless them in a very special way for their kind assistance.

May the Lord also bless this book to be used to help the babes in Christ and all those hungry and thirsty for the spiritual nourishment that comes through prayer. It is dedicated with praise and thanksgiving to the glory of God for the building of his kingdom here on earth.

—Margaret Calkin

Contents

Introduction v

CHAPTER ONE:
    Definition of Prayer 9

CHAPTER TWO:
    God Always Answers Prayer 19

CHAPTER THREE:
    Types of Prayer 31

CHAPTER FOUR:
    Beginning Methods of Prayer 47

CHAPTER FIVE:
    Hearing from the Lord 63

CHAPTER SIX:
    Praying Beyond Words 79

CHAPTER SEVEN:
    Christian Mysticism 95

CHAPTER EIGHT:
    The Laying On of Hands 113

CHAPTER NINE:
    Praying in Tongues 127

CHAPTER TEN:
    According to the Holy Spirit 141

CHAPTER ELEVEN:
    On Prayer as a Way of Life 155

CHAPTER ONE

Definition of Prayer

Dear Lord, help me to pray in accordance with your divine will and help me to help others to pray. Amen.

"My God, how do I pray? Teach me. Show me the way. Help!"

Have you ever experienced that heartfelt need? I believe every Christian has at some moment uttered that plea, especially the spiritually newborn.

What follows after a person has accepted the Lord Jesus into his or her heart? Usually that person's most immediate desire is to learn to communicate with Jesus and to understand the Lord's presence in his life! We do that through prayer, and that is why every Christian needs to learn how to pray. Therefore, the purpose of this book is to help the reader to break ground on learning how to pray.

To avoid confusion, we must first examine a basic definition of praying. *To pray is to be in communion with God, to communicate with him and to be in relationship with him.* Prayer is not something achieved through absorption, but a skill to be learned. Walking the road of prayer is a never-ending learning experience. So, how do we get started on this task? Perhaps we could take a lesson from the children.

Break Ground

Praying is an area in which I believe children may very well lead the way, because they seem to learn most easily. They keep their prayers simple and straightforward, a strong model for us adults who have become bogged down in the complications of life. These little ones have not lived long enough to clog the road with obstacles to a sweet relationship with Our Lord. They are trusting and quick to understand that Jesus loves them. Children seldom hesitate to give their hearts, minds, and souls over to the Lord and to follow him for the simple joy and pleasure of his company.

On Communication with Him

Childhood prayers are a good place to start exploring the prayer journey because they are not nearly as intimidating as "grown-up" prayers. My own experiences were simple, comforting, warm, and wonderful. Mother taught me to say "Now I lay me down to sleep. I pray the Lord my soul to keep. If I should die before I wake, I pray the Lord my soul to take." I didn't like the part about dying, but if Mother was saying it with me, it wasn't too bad. Then we did the "God bless..." routine for each member of the family, friends, pets, etc., until I could delay bed time no longer. Oh, well.

This nightly episode was a simply marvelous "warm fuzzy" in my life. I had either Mother or Daddy entirely to myself for a few minutes while we prayed to a wonderful God who was supposed to love me, watch over me while I slept, and take me to heaven if I couldn't live through the night. I didn't know what God did in the daytime, except to bless the food we ate.

It was about this time that I first knowingly experienced an immediate answer to my prayers. Also, it was my first (and so far only) experience with seeing angels.

I had gone to bed, but had not yet fallen asleep. As I tossed and turned, I repeated my formula nighttime prayer. Maybe I hoped the "God bless..." routine would lull me to

Definition of Prayer

sleep, like the counting of sheep. Regardless, I found myself stuck like glue to the "if I should die" portion of this otherwise delightful prayer. Naked fear set in! I don't remember what strategy I used (water, potty, another kiss), but I do remember my mother becoming exasperated with me and refusing to come back into the room. I'm also not sure if I was able to communicate my fear to her, or if she was simply unable to understand it. Nevertheless, I was horribly alone in my bed and rapidly approaching the brink of terror. Instinctively I reached out to God for protection, and I begged him to send angels to watch over me. When I peeked out from my covers, I found not one, but two angels standing at the foot of my bed!

"Mommy, Mommy, come see the angels!" I yelled excitedly.

"Quit playing and go to sleep, Margaret."

"I'm not playing, it's really true. Angels! Two of them."

"You are making me mad. I'm tired of your excuses. For the last time, go to sleep!"

Yet they were there! Both of them were bathed in white light. The one on the right had enormous, beautiful wings arching over his head and cascading down to his ankles; and he was dressed in a long, white, flowing robe. The other one wore a helmet, carried a shield, and was dressed in a short robe and boots. Since he didn't have wings, I had my doubts about him. I wasn't too sure there could be angels without wings. Nevertheless, my fears evaporated with my angels on duty, and eventually my excitement settled into blissful sleep. God had paused a moment in the orchestration of his universe to <u>immediately answer the prayer</u> of a small frightened child.

Even today I frequently expect an immediate answer to prayer. Perhaps it is the small child within me still trusting the Lord to help.

Often it is simply a matter of conversation with God. I

silently, but mentally talk to him. Then I wait, listening for a reply and watching for the Lord to show me the way. Many times this occurs lying in bed at the end of the day, before I drift off to sleep. Sometimes, it is in the morning before I arise to face the tasks of the day ahead. King David also found these moments to be a special time of communion and communication with our Lord. To be in communion with God means to be in spiritual fellowship with him. In his psalms, David describes lying upon his couch at night, thinking of God, sometimes praising and thanking him for blessings, sometimes simply loving and worshipping him, and sometimes complaining loudly with groaning and moaning. Regardless of the drift of the conversation, he was effectively communing with God through some pretty clear communication. In my own small way, I try to follow his example.

On Relationship with God

Knowledge about God and knowing God are not the same thing. For example, many of us know a great deal about the President of the United States, but do we really know him? Do we having a walking, talking, personal relationship with him? Think about it.

Many, many of our Christian brothers and sisters are fooled into believing that the knowledge of God gained through studying the Bible is sufficient for the day. In gaining a little theology, they can send prayers, attend worship services, and receive some comfort in times of stress. But they have really "missed the boat!" Only with humble submission to God in prayer and the commitment to receive Jesus Christ as his Lord and Savior can anyone enter into a walking, talking, personal relationship with him. Here within this personal relationship, a new spiritual life begins. Consider the following simple story of the humble beginnings of a personal relationship with the Lord.

My son Daniel had heard Bible stories about God and

Definition of Prayer

Jesus from the time we first began to read to him as a toddler. However, Jesus appeared to have been another storybook character to Dan as far as I could observe...until one famous day in early spring when Daniel was four years old.

There was a stack of plywood and boards in the backyard, the debris of tearing down our rotting porch. All of a sudden about eight little boys seemed to materialize "out of the woodwork" to pounce upon their sudden found treasure. They very quickly made a crude fort by stacking materials and leaning plywood pieces against the picket fence. I could hear all sorts of activity, commands of construction supervision, shouts of joy, arguments over the selection of wood, and loud game plans over the use of their fort. Then suddenly, total silence! As I peeked out of my kitchen window, I found all of the children had abandoned their construction site. Only Daniel was left, and he looked very sad as he entered the kitchen door.

"Daniel, what is the matter? Where are all the boys?"

"They left. There's a 'cockle roach' in my fort, and the boys won't play in it anymore."

"I am so sorry there's a bug in your fort. It's spring, and there will be lots of bugs hatching soon, so we do have a problem. As a matter of fact, if we kill the bug, there will just be more to kill later. There is only one solution that I can think of. Go find your sister Laura, and the three of us will pray together that Jesus will help us. He is the only one that I know who can solve your problem, and I know that he loves us and cares enough about you and your fort to help us."

Laura soon arrived and listened to our story. Looks of doubt passed between the two children.

"OK, you guys. Hold hands with me and with each other to form a circle while we pray." Then I used some very child-like words to speak to our Lord.

Jesus, we have a problem. Daniel has a 'cockle

roach' in his fort, and the boys don't like it, so no one will play in the fort. Please help us by getting rid of the 'cockle roach' and all the other bugs that we don't like. It might be all right to leave a lady-bug or a daddy-long-legs in the fort because we like those kinds of bugs, but the 'cockle roach' has got to go. Please help us. You are the only one who can solve our problem. Thank you very much. Amen.

Daniel ran outside to check the premises and came back ecstatically yelling, "It's gone, Mommy. It's gone!"

My husband David and I allowed the "fort" to stand for two weeks before carting the junk to the dump. During that time, we noticed all sorts of bugs emerging for spring, but NOT ONE BUG was ever found in or around the fort. This seemed to be a turning point for Daniel. He became more interested in Bible stories, and his bedtime prayers grew lively, because Jesus had become very real to him.

One night I shared this story with a class of teenagers preparing to receive the sacrament of Confirmation. Their teacher was my dear friend Mary, who had felt a nudge from the Lord to invite me to team-teach with her that night. During the session, we had particular difficulty in securing the attention of a young man I shall name Paul. It seemed Paul was always a problem in this class (as well as in school). He and several of the other teenagers were there simply because their parents had sent them, and it was the "thing to do" in church at this time of their lives. They all laughed at me and at my weird approach to religion. However, the story of the "cockle roach" interested Paul because his family was suffering an infestation of silverfish in their house. They could not seem to get rid of the bugs. As he rattled through the difficulties of pest control over these particular little beasts, I sensed that something was spiritually important about the matter, but I hesitated to ask him to pray with me then and there. So I simply mentioned that I would pray about the problem. Less than two weeks later, Paul excitedly reported to Mary by telephone that the silverfish were almost all gone! Jesus had done it again—he had secured the attention of a wayward child, touched him, and changed his life forever!

There are no standard operating procedures for entering the kingdom of God upon earth or for understanding the reality of Jesus Christ today. The Lord always finds a way to reach those who would be open to receiving him into their lives. Then he is faithful and just to uphold us in his steadfast love.

On Commitment to the Lord

How do you come to love Jesus?

Well, if you understand that he has always loved you, maybe that would help. After all, it's much easier to love someone who already loves you, someone who understands you, and someone who knows that you are a very special person—just the way you are. Many pastors would preach, "Invite Jesus into your heart and make him Lord of your life." It is called "being saved." Others would teach the same message in other terms. They would talk about asking God to come into your life in a very real way by a personal relationship with his son Jesus, because the New Testament teaches us that to know Jesus is to know the Father (John10:30). We cannot have one without the other. I like to use the term "become available to God." When I became available to God, I became available to having a personal relationship with Jesus. It didn't just happen. I had to purpose myself to follow Jesus and commit myself to being available to him. Then, since I could neither see, nor hear him, it was up to our Lord to teach me to communicate with him, to commune with him, and finally to love him with all my heart. As I began to learn to pray, I began to understand that God is love.

Actually falling in love with Jesus marks the beginning of a new life with a new love unlimited by our humanity and confined only by the holiness of spirit. No two of us who love the Lord share the same experience because each relationship is quite distinctively different. Our intimate moments are private and special, because he is the only one who has always understood me, who always will understand me, and who knows me and loves me at all times. Jesus is the only person I can love without reservation and without fear, totally and completely. It has taken me a long time to come to realize that, to become open to his love, to understand his commitment to loving me, and to believe that he will never abandon me.

In Summary, the path of prayer leads to the heart's most precious intimacy—knowing and loving Our Lord. Prayer is our means of communication with God and of bonding to him in spiritual communion. Only through the communication and communion of prayer can we develop a personal relationship with Jesus, who will always love us and who calls us to draw near to him.

Simple and straightforward prayers—heart to heart talk—can provide the most honest and profound experiences of prayer. Take lessons from the children and learn to pray in a child-like and unadorned fashion. After all, God really knows what is in your heart, so there is no need to try to impress him with fancy phrases. He loves you just the way you are. Present yourself openly and sincerely, then trust him to listen.

As we continue to learn about God, his precious son Jesus and the Holy Spirit through studying the Bible, we grow in personal relationship with the Lord and in our prayer life. You will find that the psalms of the Old Testament are among the best prayers ever written. And, in the New

Testament, Jesus taught us the Lord's Prayer (Matt. 6:9-13). Remember that prayer is not one-sided. After you speak to the Lord, take some time to listen. After all, communication involves both sending and receiving messages. Learning to pray means learning to wait upon the Lord for answers. He will teach you to hear him and to understand him.

Questions for Discussion:

1. Can you remember the first time you began to pray? Were you just a child? What were the circumstances? Who taught you about God and how to pray to him?

2. When do you feel that you are really communicating with Our Lord? Describe at least one way that you believe the Lord has spoken to you, that is, how he answered your prayer.

3. In church, at home, on the job, or during moments of relaxation, do you ever sense the Lord's presence? Have you ever shared your tears with him? Read Psalm 34:17-18.

4. Using your own words, describe your relationship to Father God, the Lord Jesus, and the Holy Spirit? Read Isaiah 43:7, 10-12. What is your commitment to this relationship? What do you think God's commitment is to you? Read Genesis 17:7 and Exodus 6:7.

5. Why is prayer the key to this relationship? Read 2 Chronicles 7:14, Psalm 145:18, and Philippians 4:6-7.

CHAPTER TWO

God Always Answers Prayer

Show them the way, Lord. Show them the way. Nothing I say will convince them. Show them the way.

Before I write another page, I must tell you that GOD ALWAYS, ALWAYS, ALWAYS ANSWERS PRAYER. Do you understand clearly? There is no doubt in my mind, body, or spirit that God always answers prayer!

There is a basic physical law that states that for every action there is a reaction. Upon this truth rests the very foundation of modern physical sciences. Likewise in the spirit, for every prayer raised to Almighty God, there is an answer to be received. Upon this truth lies the very foundation of our communication with God from which we build our relationship with him. The sooner we learn this, the better we can pray.

My daughter was only ten years old the night she challenged me, "How do I know that God hears me, Mommy? How do I know that he answers my prayers? How do I really know?"

Her need "to know" sounded most urgent, perhaps even

desperate. I could not begin to guess what childhood distress might be lurking deep within her. However, I did sense that this moment could be a turning point in her life and that my words could be critical. So I prayed my favorite unsophisticated prayer, "Lord, help me!" Then my mind cleared to understand that I must place my mustard seed of faith into her mind.

"Laura, I could spend hours talking to you about answered prayer. I could tell you all sorts of stories showing God answering my prayers and even some of yours that I can remember. But I'm not going to do that."

"Why not?"

"Because I don't think that will solve your problem. Oh, the stories would sound wonderful, maybe even exciting. But these things cannot give you what you need. I cannot give you what you truly need."

"What do you mean?"

"Only God can give you the gift of knowing that he always hears your prayers. Only he can make you know that you know that you know that you know beyond a doubt that he hears and answers you."

Then we joined hands for a short bedtime prayer which included, "Please God, show Laura very clearly that you hear her prayers and answer them. I know that you do, but she needs to know this, too."

A few minutes later I was reading in the living room when Laura bounced excitedly into the room. She was absolutely exuberant!

"Mommy, I kept thinking about our prayer, and I decided to look into the Bible like you do sometimes. See what I found when I opened it!"

She then read to me several verses of Psalm 28:

> To thee, O Lord, I call;
> my rock, be not deaf to me,

> lest, if thou be silent to me,
> > I become like those who go down to the Pit.
> >
> > Hear the voice of my supplication,
> > > as I cry to thee for help,
> >
> > as I lift up my hands
> > > toward thy most holy sanctuary.
>
> *Psalm 28:1-2 (RSV)*

> Blessed be the Lord!
> > for he has heard the voice of my supplications.
>
> The Lord is my strength and my shield;
> > in him my heart trusts;
>
> so I am helped, and my heart exults,
> > and with my song I give thanks to him.
>
> *Psalm 28:6-7 (RSV)*

"See, Mom, all I have to do is pray to him and lift my hands up like this, and he hears me, and I praise him and thank him, because I know that he will answer me. That's what this says and that's what God is showing me. Isn't it just wonderful!"

"Yes, it is wonderful; and I'm so happy for you; and I'm so grateful to the Lord for showing you the way."

All we could do was hug and kiss each other as we cuddled blissfully before the Lord with our new gift of increased faith. It seemed a long time before Laura could settle down to go to sleep that night.

In my own quiet moment of prayer, I joined the psalmist praising God and thanking him for an immediate answer to prayer.

> I give thanks, O Lord, with my whole heart;
> > before the gods I sing thy praise;
>
> I bow down toward thy holy temple
> > and give thanks to thy name for thy steadfast

love and faithfulness;
for thou hast exalted above everything
thy name and thy word.
On the day I called, thou didst answer me,
my strength of soul thou didst increase.
Psalm 138:1-3 (RSV)

The Lord knew the urgency of my young child's heart, and he responded immediately in a manner she could understand.

I lifted my own heart towards the heavens to say, "Praise you, Lord, and thank you for the privilege of watching this small miracle unfold and for these precious moments of basking in the light of your divine love."

When the Answer is No

It is easy for me to write lovely little stories about answers to prayer when the answer was joyful. It is quite another matter when the answer was not what I wanted to hear.

I must confess to the portion of my prayer life that leaves me much distressed. These are the instances in which my precious Lord says "No." I usually disagree and let him know wholeheartedly. Sometimes I even become angry with him. (What did I say? Angry with God!) Yes, to my shame, I must admit to having thrown a few temper tantrums before the Lord. I used to sort of "stuff" these feelings. After all, it seemed an outrageous heresy to be angry with God. That was supposed to be a big no-no in my life. God was all-powerful and all good, and who was I to get angry with him? On the other hand, whom was I fooling by denying my feelings? God knew I was angry, whether or not I would admit it. I eventually found out that God is even big enough to take my anger, to handle it, and to create from it new sources of light, healing, and understanding for my very soul. Praise him always.

Just yesterday I found a prayer which I had clipped out of

a newspaper, sometime and somewhere, from an author unknown to me at this point. It is entitled "Thank You, Lord, for Sometimes Saying No."

> Lord, thank you for not answering all my prayers. Most of my life I've prayed for special favors. I've pestered you for many selfish things. I've asked you to solve problems of my own creation. I have prayed that you would make life easy for me.
>
> I have prayed for sure ways to success and short cuts to material things when I should have been working to attain spiritual goals that really satisfy. I have asked you to help me understand my fellow men when I should have been listening and trying to help them with their problems.
>
> I realize now that if you had answered all my prayers, I would be weak, dependent, and perhaps lazy. By forcing me to work out some of my own problems, you have helped me to become strong.
>
> Now my days are full of opportunity to live unselfishly. That's the most important thing, which I could have prayed for.
>
> So thank you, Lord, for not giving me my every wish and refusing to answer my prayers in my way; thus, you are helping me to become the person you want me to be.

My unknown brother or sister in Christ who composed this prayer, here expresses much of my feelings regarding hindsight becoming clear insight. It usually takes me a long time to reconcile my feelings and reactions to God's negative answer. Sometimes I anguish for months and years. It seems I always have some part or portion of me that is still disagreeing with God even when my head says, "He's right. He knows what he is doing. I ought to give him credit for being a good God." I struggle to thank him for saying "no."

Nevertheless, there is an answer for every one of our prayers. It may be yes; it may be no; it may be something in-between, like wait. I keep harping on the subject because I strongly feel the need to share my faith in my God, who always answers our prayers.

The rest of this book proceeds from the unalterable basic premise that prayer is answered always. Across these pages I share my own prayer life and experiences of prayers sent with answers received, not withstanding that some of these answers made me downright uncomfortable as in the episode of my dream rabbits.

Two friends and I bubbled with excitement as we drove to Nancy's house. The three of us were rabbit breeders, and we were on our way to inspect a new breed called Holland lops. We had read about them and seen pictures of them, but knew of none within driving distance until Nancy's advertisement appeared in the local newspaper. She was breeding Holland lops and offering a few for sale. Although we felt intrigued by these animals, none of us were considering a purchase at this time because the rabbits cost $100 each (too expensive for our slim pocketbooks)! But we could dream and look and ask questions.

While we were looking at the rabbits, I understood the Lord nudging me to place a $50 deposit on a female (doe) baby bunny. Since this was not a part of my plans, I did not particularly want to hear the message.

I mentally debated, "Lord, if I hear you clearly, you are telling me to leave a $50 deposit on a baby rabbit. You know that I'm going on vacation next week. My family needs every penny I've got. As it is, I don't think we have quite enough money for our vacation."

Silence.

"Are you really sure you want me to buy this rabbit?"

"Yes."

"Are you really very, very sure you want me to buy this rabbit?"

"Yes."

After a long hesitation, I capitulated. "I don't like it, Lord, but I will do it. You will have to stretch my vacation funds. OK?"

"OK."

Then I took a deep breath and tried to calmly announce my "decision" to leave a deposit towards purchasing one of the rabbits.

Nancy quickly asked, "Which one?"

Her question caught me off guard. I had been so busy internally grumping and arguing with the Lord that I had not yet thought about which bunny. Feeling a bit foolish, I admitted that I needed to pray for a few minutes to make my decision. Although she gave me a strange look, Nancy accepted my answer without comment and left me alone with the rabbits.

After I had selected my bunny and written the deposit check, one of my friends asked, "Margaret, why did you choose that specific animal?"

I felt cornered.

To honestly answer her question, I would have to bear witness to God's involvement in my life. It was a moment of truth and an open door for sharing Jesus Christ as Lord in my life. It was also an opportunity to become a fool for Christ, because I felt quite vulnerable to their ridicule and laughter. Was I going to acknowledge Jesus here and now, or was I going to hide him through excuses, evasive answers, or silence?

Break Ground

I reluctantly confessed, "The Lord told me to buy that bunny. It was not my idea. I had not planned this." Mentally I threatened to add, "It's all his fault!"

Obviously, I did not feel very confident about sharing my thoughts with these women. However, they seemed to accept what I was saying without much comment. It was the beginning of their long-term observation of me praying over rabbits.

The following week our family went on a vacation that turned out blessedly free of economic pain. For this I give credit to the Lord for stretching our money with grocery sales, discount tickets and free recreation. It must have part of his plan for us all along.

Shortly after returning home, I was able to complete the payment and to pick up my baby doe. At that time, I informed Nancy I would eventually need a buck (male rabbit) for breeding purposes. Otherwise, I would lose the best baby in each litter as the "pick of the litter" stud service fee. I intended to start saving money immediately to purchase the buck, which I reasoned was part of God's plan for me. But, I was wrong. The next part of God's plan for me was a complete surprise.

Nancy called me a few weeks later with shocking news. She was selling all of her stock because she had decided to quit rabbit breeding. There remained a fine breeding trio of two does and one buck. Was I interested in buying them? I certainly was interested in buying the buck, but she was only open to a group sale. I asked the price and gasped at her answer—$300. I told her I would think about it and call her back.

"Help, Lord!" I was beginning to panic because Nancy was my only resource for Holland lops.

Then I began to pray, "Lord, what do you want me to do?"

"Buy the rabbits."

"You've got to be kidding, Lord. Where do I get the money?"

About that time, my friend Jocelyn arrived at my doorstep, and I told her what was happening. After she prayed with me for guidance, the message seemed clear.

"You heard me, Margaret, buy the rabbits."

"OK, Lord. What do I use for money?"

I suddenly remembered a small stack of checks that I had received over the past few weeks in payment of some used cages and a few baby bunnies that I had sold out of the minilops and Netherland dwarf rabbits I had been breeding. I kept feeling a need to save these small amounts of money. Now I knew why. I counted $90, a good start on the $300 that I needed.

"Well, Lord, where is the rest of it?"

"In your emergency fund."

"But, Lord," I argued, "you know that I'm not supposed to touch that money, except for family emergencies. Are you sure you want me to use some of that money?"

"Yes."

"I don't like this, Lord. I don't like this at all."

Silence.

Moan, groan, struggle! I had to decide whether or not to obey my God. This meant putting aside my own rules and regulations, plus trusting the Lord with my treasured funds. Jocelyn seemed to be my appointed intercessor for the situation. I knew she was praying; she knew I knew she was praying; and I thanked God that she was praying. She also offered to help me by following me in her car so that we would have two cars to transport cages and rabbits home. Actually her offering of help contributed to my feelings of being cornered.

Reluctantly I agreed, "Lord, I'll do it; I still don't like it; but I will do it. I'm feeling terribly uncomfortable in this situation. However, you must have a plan that I do not understand; and I have decided to obey you."

After a quick telephone call to confirm the arrangements,

Break Ground

Jocelyn and I drove to the bank to withdraw money and then we proceeded to Nancy's house. I was so upset that I didn't even realize that I was "crawling" at a snail's pace of 40 mph on the highway in the middle of high-speed traffic. Jocelyn laughed because she had never seen me drive so slowly on the open highway.

With distress written all over my face, I reluctantly purchased the rabbits and negotiated the purchase of some used caging for an additional $35. Jocelyn was praying the whole time. She helped me to load both cars before we returned home with my leading at an even slower pace. Upon arrival, we unloaded Jocelyn's car, and she went home—still praying. Then I made some telephone calls. I had not even unpacked my car before I had sold all of the cages and possibly one of the rabbits. By nightfall I had received $60 for the cages. Two days later I received $120 for one of the does (already bred). I was able to return all of the borrowed money to my emergency kitty within 72 hours! By the end of the week, I had sold the remaining cages for sufficient funds to complete my transaction with Nancy without any loss from my household accounts. The Lord had done it again! All I had to do was to use his strength to obediently follow his directives. It was a lesson that I hope to never forget.

However, I had found all of these events so distressing and so painful that it was one entire week later before I realized that these rabbits were an answer to my prayer of the year before. Yes, I suddenly remembered the night I was lying in bed reviewing a rabbit magazine when I discovered a picture of Holland lops. I sort of just fell in love with these rabbits right away and mentioned it to my husband, David.

He said, "Why don't you buy one?"

I answered, "Because they cost too much. I doubt that I could even find one of very poor quality for less than $125."

Since he understood the price was beyond our budget, David dropped the subject. Still admiring the picture, I thought, "Lord, you know I would love to have one of those rabbits." Then I, too, dropped the subject and eventually forgot about it. However, the Lord did not forget. He planned and timed it perfectly to give me my heart's desire and more. With a trio of excellent quality breeding stock, I found myself raising Holland lops—my dream rabbits.

In Summary, we are assured through the Holy Scriptures that our loving God hears our prayers and even knows our every thought before we utter a word to him. He never sleeps, nor abandons his loving watch over us for even a moment. As we learn to pray, we learn to trust that Our Lord will answer us. Sometimes the answer becomes quite apparent as a "yes" or a "no." Often it is not quite so easy to understand anything as an answer. Many people have fallen into the habit of sending prayer as a message to the Lord without taking time to listen for an answer or to observe the changing circumstances of their lives as an answer to the prayer. Spiritual listening takes practice. It is then that our faith is tested as we must put our trust in him and learn to wait upon the Lord, for his answer always comes within his perfect timing and in his perfect plan—not ours. More about this in Chapter Five.

Questions for Discussion:

1. Have you ever felt completely frustrated when you are praying, as if you are not sure that God is listening? King David had the same problem, often expressed in the psalms as pleading with the Lord to give ear to him and listen to his cries for help. Reference Psalms 4:1, 5:2, 28:2, and 64:1 for just a few examples.

2. King David also wrote psalms of praise and thanksgiving to acknowledge that God had heard his prayers and come

Break Ground

to the rescue. Read Psalms 10:17, 22:24, and 31:22. Have you ever felt that your prayer was answered and that you were kept safe from harm by divine intervention? If so, did you take time to praise and to thank the Lord for his blessing? If not, take a moment to do so now.

3. Take a few minutes to ask Jesus to bring to your mind a recent answer to prayer that you may not have noticed. If you do this each day, you may be amazed at the results!

4. If you are in a group study, share a "yes" answer to one of your prayers. Remember that God will use your gratitude and your witness to help build up the faith in others.

5. Now think about a "no" answer to prayer. You may or may not want to share the experience, but remember that God uses all things for our good. Read Romans 8:28, Genesis 50:20, and Isaiah 38:17.

6. Have you ever become angry with God for not answering your prayers as you desired? Did you tell the Lord how you felt? Were you ashamed to be angry with God and did you try to hide your feelings? Read Psalm 139:1-13 as a reminder that the Lord knows us intimately and that we cannot hide from him. Then read Jeremiah 29:11.

CHAPTER THREE

Types of Prayer

Lord, you know I don't want to sound "preachy"; so please direct me to introduce types of prayer without seeming pontifical. Thank you very much.

During my explorations of prayer I have discovered several ways to categorize the types of prayer. More than one person has suggested the memory trick of ACTS: Adoration, Contrition, Thanksgiving, and Supplication. You might want to use this method; however, you would also need to remember praise as a portion of the thanksgiving prayer and intercession as a component of the supplication prayer. In reflecting upon my own life experiences of learning to pray, I encountered the following types of prayer in the sequence here listed:

1. Supplication
2. Intercession
3. Praise and thanksgiving
4. Adoration

When I presented this list to my pastor, he responded, "What happened to contrition?" Well, I have chosen to view contrition as a part of supplication. You may not agree with me. Go right ahead—you have my full permission to have your own opinion!

On Supplication

Supplication. What a big word, almost intimidating! The word *supplication* means to beg (a person) humbly and earnestly. Consequently, I have trouble accepting the notion of sincere begging without humility because without humility, supplication simply becomes a "gimme prayer." "Lord, gimme success, gimme your favor, gimme what I want when I want it...."

Without humility, the problem of the ego becomes a tremendous obstacle in learning how to pray. Most of us carry around a mountain of emotional garbage, like jealousy, bitterness, self-centeredness, and pride. This junk prevents people from truly humbling themselves to sincerely present their petitions to a Holy God.

Usually children have little trouble learning prayers of supplication to a heavenly God they can trust. "Now I lay me down to sleep..." and "bless this food..." begin the simple prayers we teach our children with their trusting hearts. Their unadulterated hearts eagerly accept the basic message, "Jesus loves me."

I can remember my own childhood as a time of believing in miracles based on simple faith and little understanding. Pure trust in the Lord! Then the emotional garbage set in and the level of trust receded. What happened? I "grew up!" I learned to pray and then to figure out my answers as best I could. I was not taught to wait upon the Lord for answers to my prayers, except for recognizing the evolution of circumstances, which were often labeled "luck." I got stuck in the "help-me-God" syndrome with pleas for mercy only when I couldn't manage my life successfully without divine intervention.

To avoid an unhealthy guilt trip over the help-me-God

Types of Prayer

syndrome, I must consider one thing. It was a beginning. I was looking for God in my simple, rudimentary manner, even if it was mostly "crunch" situations. And, God in his steadfast love for me was faithful; he did not turn away, nor hide his face from me. Jesus was true to his word:

> All that the Father giveth me shall come to me; and him that cometh to me I will in no wise cast out.
> *John 6:37 (KJV)*

Did you hear that promise loud and clear? Through the precious son Jesus, our God promises us he will never cast us out or drive us away when we humble ourselves to seek his face. NEVER, NEVER, NEVER! His love and mercy is not contingent upon what we deserve or feel that we may have earned.

There are so many times the Lord has baffled me with his loving kindness, especially when I think I've begun to "know it all." My ego demands periodic adjustment, and my Lord faithfully attends to this need without request. In other words, I find myself humbled. If I will look beyond the surface and listen for his voice, he will guide me and lovingly teach me of his mercy and his ways.

In his own simple and childish manner, my son Daniel became a witness to the mercy of Jesus Christ. From the beginning of first grade through his fourth grade year, Daniel could never get organized in the morning before school. No matter how early we wakened him, nor how much time he had to dress, breakfast, and prepare for school, he always managed to be unprepared for the arrival of the school bus. I would hear him suddenly shout "Oh, no! I'm going to miss my bus. Jesus, help me! Jesus! Jesus! Help! Jesus!" Then he would run around panic stricken as he collected his loose ends before dashing out the door.

One day I made the mistake of "correcting him." I told

him that he couldn't pray like that. He was asking God to save him from the consequences of his own bad habits without ever trying to correct them. I told him that one day God was not going to continue to honor his pleas for help, not until he had gotten his act together by at least trying to get better organized and out of the door on time.

Then the Lord asked, "Margaret, who are you to tell him when I will and when I will not answer prayer. Are you God?"

I felt mortified.

Thank goodness, Daniel ignored my spiritual guidance and continued to yell for Jesus to save him every morning. The Lord was blessedly steadfast in his faithfulness to rescue Daniel. He orchestrated a little miracle every morning, sometimes even stalling the school bus in mid-motion on the road, so that my son never missed that bus. And, I believe that Jesus did this to *teach me* a lesson!

Aside from the pleas of mercy during times of crisis, there is another circumstance in which I can readily understand supplication as an act of earnest begging in all humility. It is the appropriate attitude for contrition (also known as confession). When I know that I have sinned and I understand the need for repentance, there is no circumventing a sincere begging for God's forgiveness. I praise and thank him for his forgiveness and his precious mercy flowing down upon my soul. However, I must remember that no one, especially God, absolutely has to forgive me for my transgressions. Although the Lord promises us forgiveness when we repent, it is not my unequivocal right to be forgiven, and I must suffer an attitude adjustment if I ever assume forgiveness without sincere and humble repentance. Forgiveness, both from God and from other persons, is a gift to be received with gratitude. It is an act of love to which we must learn to respond in love. I learned this lesson when my daughter Laura was a teenager.

One weekend my husband David and I enjoyed an

Types of Prayer

overnight vacation trip, leaving our teenage children at home by themselves. Household rules prohibited the children from having guests in our absence. When I returned, however, I discovered evidence in the garbage can of a party as I was disposing of trash. Although I was disturbed, I said nothing to anyone. An hour later I discovered a foreign gold earring on the carpet in my bedroom. Shortly thereafter, Laura came home from a group outing and cheerfully bounced into my bedroom to have a lovely little chat. I asked a few vague questions about her weekend, making sure that everything went well, especially with her younger brother. Her answers included nothing to indicate that friends had stopped by.

As she was leaving the room, I handed her the earring and casually remarked, "Look what I found on the rug near my bed."

Looking a bit startled, she practically snatched the earring from my hand, quickly examined it, and with head still down looking at the earring, she proceeded up the stairs with a mumbled, "Oh, great, I was wondering where this had been." She averted her gaze from me because we both knew the earring belonged to someone else.

I waited. A barrier of deception had arisen between us. For two miserable days, we were unable to be joyfully spontaneous in our relationship as mother and child.

As I was washing dishes a couple of days later, Laura came home from school, pecked a kiss on my cheek as she said hello, then started to leave the kitchen. But, she just couldn't go away and keep pretending everything was OK.

"Mother, I have to tell you something. You probably know—no, I know you know—that I had company while you and Dad were gone. Actually I had some people over for a small party," she blurted in a rush of words.

"I'm sorry and I won't ever do that again."

I was thrilled and rushed to hug her with soapy wet hands. "Laura, I'm so glad you told me. I've felt like there was a shadow between us and now it's gone. Thank God!"

Then she began to tell me the details: how she got rid of little brother, coordinated the logistics of the party, and had a wonderful time with her friends. She thought she had cleaned up and covered her tracks pretty well. There was only a vastly diminished pang of guilt buried at the back of her mind until I unearthed the lost golden earring. She then swam into the deeper waters of deception with her cover-up comments, and she tarnished our relationship in the process.

We both realized more clearly how sin can open chasms between people and casts soil upon the bonds of love. Consequently, I gratefully experienced a new dimension in the joy of forgiveness when my daughter confessed her error and said she was sincerely sorry for having deceived me. It just felt wonderful to have our relationship "set right" again.

Suddenly I could better understand why we must humble ourselves before God and beg his forgiveness for our sins. God does not relish bringing us to our knees in repentance. It's a painful affair. However, God knows it is the only way we can "set right" our relationship with him in order to commune with him in the purity of love and the Holy Spirit. Confession is not only good for the soul, it is the remedy which returns us to health and wholeness with our one and only God.

On Intercession

The second form of prayer I learned as a young child was intercession. Very simply stated, intercession means to pray for someone else. The appendage to "Now I lay me down to sleep..." was the "God bless Mommy and Daddy and Sister and puppy and Grandma and Grandpa and dolly and teddy and...and...and..." until forced to terminate with a great big AMEN, which abruptly ended my delaying tactics for bed time. Nevertheless, I had begun to learn to pray for others, not just for myself. And I wonder, even today, if some of the

Types of Prayer

most powerful prayers I offer may simply be to ask God to bless someone.

As I ventured through childhood in the Roman Catholic Church, I learned mostly to pray by format. That is, I memorized the prayers and recited them according to formula like the rosary or according to the appropriate liturgical occasion. I did learn to offer these prayers for other people, but I never considered myself as an intercessor. That was a job appropriated to the canonical saints, who knew how to talk to God on behalf of us undeserving and unimportant people. So I spent years, asking saint such-and-such to pray for me and saint so-and-so to pray for those whom I loved and cared about. I was a mature married woman with two young children and worshipping as an Episcopalian before I learned to pray directly to Our Lord without inhibitions, especially in the matter of intercession for others.

How did I learn? How did I break ground on intercession? Believe it or not, it started with a list of people in need of prayer.

When I discovered a local Christian tape ministry, I found their people began the business day with prayer. In addition to prayers for guidance in the ministry, they prayed for many people who had requested their prayer support. That list kept growing longer and they needed help. Eventually I joined the prayer group and prayed with them whenever possible. I also committed myself to pray daily for a list of ten people with specific requests. By listening to my prayer partners, I learned to speak very simple prayers on behalf of others.

"Lord, Jessica's baby is in the hospital. Please bring healing to the child and help the doctors and nurses who treat her. Help Jessica and the rest of her family in this time of stress."

"Lord, George is worried about his exams. Please help him to study. Carry him when he is too weary to continue. Thank you, Lord."

"Bob is a troubled child, Lord. His parents just don't know

how to handle him any more. Teach them to parent their child as you would parent him. Somehow find a way to let him know how much he is loved. Bring peace to the family."

Through these daily intercessory prayers, I felt myself drawing nearer to God. I felt like a child sloshing around a golden waterfall of grace and mercy. Whenever the ministry received news that a prayer was answered, I felt so blessed, so grateful to my sweet Jesus and so very excited. For the first time in my life I focused upon the answers to my prayer as well as the petition. My faith bloomed and grew and grew and grew as I learned to expect answers in God's perfect timing and in his perfect way. In the epistle of James we are exhorted to "pray for one another, so that you may be healed. The prayer of the righteous is powerful and effective" (James 5:16-17, NRSV). In this work of prayer we love God and our fellow man according to the greatest commandments. It's not just "the nice Christian thing to do"; it is life support for one another.

Have you ever realized how difficult, if not downright impossible it may be for a person in distress to pray for himself or herself? In the midst of suffering physical pain, mental anguish or spiritual oppression, a person may not be able to even think clearly, much less pray. Those are the occasions of intercession when we need to be held in prayer by others. It is not the season for self-help or boot-strapping out of problems. Since I have learned this simple truth, I no longer suffer as much. Whenever "the going gets tough" in any dimension of my life, I call a loving prayer partner or two or three and "the tough [prayer warriors] get going." And God is faithful to answer those prayers. I am never alone in my pain, unless I choose to be.

On Praise and Thanksgiving

This morning when I watered my plants, I stopped a moment to praise the Lord and thank him for my elegant

Types of Prayer

fuschia in glorious full bloom. I paused to note how easy it was to praise him and thank him for his creation when I looked upon a sunny morning with a lovely cool breeze caressing my forehead. How difficult it is to even think of praising God or thanking him for anything in the middle of the storms of life. Yet he is the same Lord always, our God in the depths of tribulation as well as the seasons of rejoicing. Faithful to us. Loving us. Grieving with us.

Remember, God so loves us that he gave his only begotten son Jesus to show the way to eternal life and to pay the price for us by dying for our sins. For that alone we should praise him and thank him under all circumstances.

The transition from an attitude of "woe is me" to the understanding of Jesus standing by my side and crying with me over my pain was a life changing moment. It did not change the external circumstances of my distress or my feelings of being misunderstood and rejected. But when I sensed the presence of Jesus and his tears, I was first amazed, then overwhelmed by his love for me. I felt comforted and my hurt began to diminish. I try to remember that moment and cling to it in my times of distress. It is not always possible. I'm only human.

We are taught throughout the Old Testament and the New Testament that our God is the one and only true God and worthy to be praised.

> The Lord is my rock, my fortress and my deliverer
>   my God, my rock in whom I take refuge,
>   my shield, and the horn of my salvation, my
>   stronghold.
> I call upon the Lord, who is worthy to be praised,
>   so I shall be saved from my enemies
> *Psalm 18:2-3 (NRSV)*

Throughout the psalms, King David repeatedly blesses

the Lord, praises him and thanks him for his love, his mercy and gift of salvation.

This theme of praising God and thanking him continues throughout Holy Scripture to include the Apostle Paul's epistle to the Philippians.

> ...Fix your thoughts on what is true and good and right. Think about things that are pure and lovely, and dwell on the fine, good things in others. Think about all you can praise God for and be glad about.
> *Phil. 4:8 (TLB)*

Praising God is perhaps the most powerful road of thought to the gratitude that we should feel for the gifts of God. However, God does not want us to feel grateful for his sake. Whether or not we are grateful does not hurt God, it hurts us. It is in within the realization of gratitude that we become aware of how very much we are loved. As we understand the hand of God upon even the smallest events of our lives, we grow closer to him, and the bonds of love are strengthened.

On Adoration

It is the building of personal relationship with the Lord and the consequential bonding in love to him which opens the door to adoration, the highest form of love.

> And thou shalt love the Lord thy God with all thine heart, and with all thy soul, and with all thy might.
> *Deut. 6:5 (KJV)*

Loving means relationship and intimacy with the beloved; and we are instructed through Holy Scripture to love God. We are commanded to draw into an intimate relationship

Types of Prayer

with our God. How does this happen?

In the Old Testament our God had an entirely different relationship to us, his children upon earth. It bespoke of clouds of dust, walls of water, Mosaic law—a God that could hardly be approached by the little people like you and me. That sounds a little bit scary, doesn't it? Burning bushes and rivers of blood. However among all of these books shines the hope of a savior, a messiah, the Son of God, who will deliver us from our sins and show us the way to new life.

Once as a substitute teacher, I asked our third grade Sunday school students, "Why would God need to send Jesus to earth?"

They more or less responded, "...to show us the way to live good lives so we wouldn't wind up being bad people."

"That really doesn't answer my question. God had already given us a bunch of laws known as the Ten Commandments to show us how he wants us to live. We can be nice people without knowing Jesus Christ. After all, lots of people understand that it is wrong to kill other people, to lie, to steal, and to cheat. Lots of people work very hard trying to live according to these commandments which God gave us thousands of years before the birth of Christ."

Yes, they seemed to understand the Mosaic Law, and they pointed proudly to the construction paper tablets they had made and tacked to the wall in previous classes.

"If we already have all the rules to show us how to be good people, why do we need Jesus?"

Blank faces. Suddenly a light shined through the mental darkness as one little boy asked, "What about love?"

"That's it! That's the magic word, LOVE! You are absolutely right. What about love? Have you ever loved someone because you were told to?"

"No."

"Yet, we are instructed by the first commandment to love God. We are also instructed to love our neighbors and to love and honor our parents. Loving our parents is usually the easy part. But, did you ever love a neighborhood kid or a classmate just because a grownup like your teacher said you had to love them?"

"No."

"Then how do you really expect folks to love God just because they were told to love him according to the Law of Moses? Rules and regulations don't really mean you automatically love a person. It takes spending time with a person and getting to know him before you can love him. When you meet another person at school, doesn't it take time playing with him, working with him, and talking to him to become just friends? So how can you love God just because the Bible says so?"

Perplexity personified. Then several mental light bulbs seemed to pop on all at once and eyes lit up. The dawn of a new age!

"Jesus," answered one child.

"Yes, Jesus," agreed another and another.

"You are right. It is through Jesus that we can learn to love God because it is only by coming to know Jesus that we come to know God. And, it is only by loving Jesus that we can obey all those Mosaic laws because we love God."

This small, but profound lesson is not confined to the young ears of the Sunday school classroom. It is a truth and a treasure of the heart.

Loving our God and the Lord Jesus is the foundation of adoration. One simply cannot adore without love. Prayerful adoration includes worship and reverence of the one true God to be loved above all else.

I personally don't believe any person can just decide to enact a prayer of adoration. It's just not a decision-making event. Adoration evolves from love, which evolves from intimate personal relationship to God through his son Jesus. This takes time and purposing our hearts to commitment. It

Types of Prayer

seldom happens overnight. So, be patient with yourself if you have not yet experienced sincere adoration in your prayer life.

My own limited experience of adoration has proven to be a peak emotional event as well as the highest spiritual form of prayer I've ever known. It is not the point of beginning or ending of a prayer, but a mountain top experience I can only sustain for a very short time, maybe just a few minutes. Adoration of the Lord is all consuming with intensity which my body and soul can only survive in small increments. It creeps upon me usually after I have spent a significant amount of time in praise and thanksgiving. It is the next spiral upward as I reach to the Lord with all my being. Along with the creatures in Revelation, I sing, "Holy, holy, holy, the Lord God the Almighty who was and is and is to come." (Rev. 4:8, NRSV). And, my soul joins those elders as

...they cast their crowns before the throne, singing,

'You are worthy, our Lord and God,
   to receive glory and honor and power,
for you created all things,
   and by your will they existed
     and were created.'
Rev. 4:11 (NRSV)

Then I must come down slowly, and a bit sadly, having known a moment of the glory of God beyond time and space. Still praising and thanking him for all things, I descend to my little world here on earth, a bit changed forever more. I feel humbled and peaceful and stilled to the depths of my being.

In Summary, there is a type of prayer to meet our every need. Jesus encourages us to ask God prayerfully for whatever we desire. He said that his Father in heaven wants to give us good gifts. In the simple prayer of supplication, we admit our wants and ask the Lord to help us. One aspect of this is the act of contrition—a repentant heart in the humble confession of sin, ending with a plea for God's forgiveness. The sinner often needs to ask forgiveness also from the person he has wronged. These prayerful acts are necessary to "set the relationship right" between the Lord and the sinner.

After learning to pray in supplication for ourselves, it becomes a logical next step to pray for other people. Prayers of intercession are the means by which we hold each other up and stand in the gap between the person who needs help and the beloved Lord God who would give mercy and bestow amazing grace. The prayer of praise and thanksgiving proves more than a simple "thank you" to God for all he has given. I believe it is the most powerful form of prayer, because praise and thanksgiving becomes the primary form of that worship which enthrones the Lord upon our hearts (Psalm 22:3, NIV).

Praise and thanksgiving abides in the path to adoration, the most intimate form of prayer. Adoration of God is a spiritual act of love that defies description by mere words. It lifts us to sublime light of exalting, worshipping, and adoring God for who he is—our creator, redeemer, and sanctifier. The prayer of adoration is a mountaintop experience gifted to us by the Holy Spirit with whom and through whom we ultimately meet with the Lord.

Questions for Discussion:

1. In the parable of the Pharisee and the tax collector (Luke 18:10-14), Jesus gave us an example the self-righteous and pompous approach to God in contrast to a humble attitude toward prayer. Can you sincerely pray for humility, and can you give God the glory for all you have done?

Types of Prayer

2. The prayer of supplication is simply a humble request of something for ourselves. Read Matthew 7:7-11

3. The Apostle Paul knew full well the value and the need for intercessors. Read Ephesians 6:18-19 and 1 Tim. 2:1-4. How much time do you spend interceding for others? It's a great way to kick the poor-little-old-me-I-need-help-and-pity syndrome!

4. Read the fifteenth chapter of Luke to rediscover the joy of heaven over the return of just one sinner. Discuss the parable of the prodigal son with emphasis upon the restoration of relationships.

5. Take a moment right now just to praise the Lord and thank him for all things large and small, to wonder at his reservoir of unending mercies, and to acknowledge him in the smallest details of your life. Read Psalm 111 and 116 as two examples of praise and thanksgiving.

6. The prayer of adoration comes eventually to all of those who love the Lord and spend time with him. Pray now to attain the true understanding of spiritual adoration.

CHAPTER FOUR

Beginning Methods of Prayer

Lord, you have taught me many ways to pray. It seems to be a lifetime learning experience. As you have sent others to teach me, so let my words teach others. Guide my thoughts and my pen to be pleasing works in your sight. Amen.

On Corporate Prayer

Methods of prayer can be divided primarily into corporate prayer and individual prayer. By corporate prayer, I mean prayer in unity with other people versus praying alone. Christians are called to pray together and for one another as a family—the family of God composed of the people of God. We are called to love one another as ourselves for the love of Our Lord, and this cannot be accomplished in isolation with denial of relationship to each other or to the community of worship.

Corporate prayer can be formal or informal. By formal, I am referring to standardized formats of prayer as is common in the Sunday church service of most denominations. Many times these services become holy events of monumental spiritual movement among the congregation, that is, when they are truly in union and communion with the Lord. (Unfortunately, this is not always the case because services can degrade to simple ritual and format without true worship.)

Informal corporate prayer occurs whenever two or more people gather in the name of the Lord to pray. It can happen under any circumstances and in any place at any time. It simply means that more than one person is agreeing to the same prayer.

Some of the most powerful spiritual events of my own life have occurred during informal corporate prayer at Bible study or in prayer meetings. The Lord is always present in corporate prayer just as he taught us "...where two or three are gathered together in my name, there I am in the midst of them." (Matt. 18:20, RSV) Remember those words the next time you reach out to pray with someone, even as casually as to bless the lunch you may be sharing.

On Individual Prayer

Although corporate prayer is necessary to balance the prayer life in the Christian, it is the individual or personal methods of prayer I wish to address more explicitly. There are probably as many ways to pray as there are people who do the praying, because prayer largely reflects upon the individual's relationship or non-relationship to God. There are no restrictions or qualifications for the applicant to prayer. <u>God listens to each of us at all times under all circumstances.</u> He is quite comfortable in communicating with us. However, it is up to each one of us to learn to be comfortable with prayer to him.

A great starting point for most people is the use of prayers that have been previously composed by other people. The most beloved, well-known, and totally powerful prayer in Christian life came from Jesus himself when he gave us The Lord's Prayer:

Beginning Methods of Prayer

> ...Our Father which art is heaven, Hallowed be thy name. Thy kingdom come, Thy will be done in earth, as it is in heaven. Give us this day our daily bread. And forgive us our debts, as we forgive our debtors. And lead us not into temptation, but deliver us from evil: For thine is the kingdom, and the power, and the glory, for ever. Amen.
> *Matt. 6:9-13 (KJV)*

You can find inspirational works of contemplation, meditation and prayer in any Christian bookstore. Many regular bookstores and libraries also contribute a great resource. Some churches have published their own prayer books, liturgy, breviaries, and lectionaries for additional guidance. The important point is to find something that feels right for you and use it!

There can be great comfort in reading a prayer and utilizing it for yourself, especially if you are having trouble expressing your thoughts in prayerful petition to the Lord. To that end I offer the following prayer (my gift to you) to be used if it should fit the desires of your heart.

> Dear Lord, teach me to pray. Show me the way to your heart. Let me hear your voice and learn to understand your guidance. I want to become more aware of your presence and to feel your hand upon every portion of my life. Teach me to see clearly the answers to my prayers, whether or not I like them, and to know that you have only my best interests in your heart. Teach me how to praise you and to thank you for all the circumstances of my life and how to rest in your Love and to know your peace which surpasses my understanding. Amen.

Although he will always know your heart, it can be also

important for you to clarify your own thinking to better understand your own prayer.

On Personalizing the Word

Another simple and effective method of prayer is to use sections of the Bible, substituting yourself for the historical author of the words. I have found special inspiration and direction for prayer in the Book of Psalms. Try it. Read the following verses as if they are your own words addressed to the Lord.

> O Lord, you have searched me and known me,
> You know when I sit down and when I rise up;
> > you discern my thoughts from far away.
>
> You search out my path and my lying down,
> > and are acquainted with all my ways.
>
> Even before a word is on my tongue,
> > O Lord, you know it completely.
>
> You hem me in, behind and before,
> > and lay your hand upon me.
>
> Such knowledge is too wonderful for me;
> > it is so high that I cannot attain it.
>
> *Psalm 139:1-6 (NRSV)*

This may appear like pure plagiarism, but rest assured, the Lord is pleased to hear from you with borrowed words, especially if they are from Holy Scripture. There are thousands of verses to explore as you break ground on learning how to pray. There is something applicable to every circumstance of life.

I encourage Bible browsing for inspiration, meditation, and prayer. Often I seem to "hear from God" as I browse through the pages of scripture, stopping to read segments almost at random. Sometimes words seem to leap from the page at me, and I have to pause and think upon them and wonder exactly how they might apply to me at that time. Many times I find those words just what I needed to hear. It happens too often to be a coincidence, so I choose to label it amazing grace. I thank God and praise him for finding another way to commune with me.

Holy Scripture is a primary source of communication with the Lord. Not only is it an excellent resource for written prayer, but the Bible teaches us knowledge of God so that we may conform our hearts and our prayers to the Holy Spirit.

On Prayer Guarantees

I have a small list of what I consider to be "absolute guarantees" for prayer. Don't laugh. They always work, at least they always work for me. And, maybe you would also like to try them.

First on my list is a guarantee which came directly from Jesus as he taught the disciples.

> Again, truly I tell you, if two of you agree on earth about anything you ask, it will be done for you by my Father in heaven. For where two or three are gathered in my name, I am there among them.
> *Matt. 18:19-20 (NRSV)*

When I first read these words, I thought, "This is too good to be true!" Jesus promises us his presence in corporate prayer, and he promises us answers! However, if I try just a little bit to believe that Jesus loves me, then it must be pretty logical that he would want to support me in prayer. This continues to be a challenge for me to accept, although time after time the Lord proves to me that his words remains true. I remember relying on his promise one Christmas Eve.

It had been one of those awful flu seasons when everybody

in the household had been sick. You know the scene...we just kept passing the "bugs" around. My daughter Laura was about ten years old, and she dearly loved the children's Christmas service. Even though she felt unwell and <u>she could barely talk</u>, she begged me to take her to church. I agreed to take her if she was without fever by afternoon. Consequently, she and I were able to make the service, although we left little brother (and his sniffles) at home with Daddy.

Part way through the service, Laura asked me if I thought Baby Jesus would heal her. She was so tired of feeling miserable and not being able to talk and play. I told her that he certainly could make her well again, and I agreed to join her in asking him to do so. We bowed our heads in silent prayer together. Then I whispered to her that something might happen at the communion rail because our Lord comes to meet us there in a very special way.

She must have gone forward expecting her little miracle. Not only did she return to the pew with a smile on her face, <u>she was able to sing</u> the final hymn! We had prayed together in the Lord's presence and according to his will.

The second guarantee on my list is that God will conform a person's will to his own, if that person grants him permission to do so. Using the imagery of the potter and the clay, one submits to the Lord to be molded and created into new life. However, just as the lump of clay cannot tell the potter what to make, remember that you are giving the Lord control over your life, you are willing to do and to be whatever he desires, whether or not you like the idea. Of course, the answer to the prayer is also the answer to any dilemma you may have over the Lord's will because eventually your own will becomes the same as his. This is sometimes a painful process; nevertheless, it is always rewarding.

I am reminded of the story of the pastor who recognized his need for increased patience as he attended to the leadership problems of his congregation. He knew that it was the

Lord's will for him to grow in this area of his life, and he knew that it would be a difficult task. Nevertheless, he reluctantly submitted himself to the Lord to conform his will to God's calling to learn patience. Of course, his prayer was answered.

The following week, the extraordinarily competent and very loving church secretary (who had been there for years) resigned suddenly to move with her husband to a new job in another state. The new secretary proved to be neither as competent, nor as loving and understanding of the pastor's impatience and outbursts of irritability. The office work slowed down and often had to be redone. In the midst of this mountain of aggravation, insight came as the pastor realized that the Lord was teaching him patience because the situation demanded far more patience than he had ever achieved in his entire life. Everyday became a day to lean on the Lord for patience, and gradually increased patience came. Along with it came the unexpected blessings of nurturing another person into the bloom of personal growth and development. As the pastor became more patient, the secretary became more competent. Irritability and aggravation vanished to be replaced by gratitude and humble thanksgiving to the Lord for answered prayer.

Finally, I have two very short prayers to add to my list of guarantees. The first prayer is simply, "Lord, have mercy on me." Whether the answer is yes or no or something in between, the Lord always, always, always has mercy upon his children who trust in him and call upon him for help.

I once had a friend (I'll call Robert) who continuously misused his business credit card for personal applications. At the end of the fiscal year he needed to balance the account with the company, and he was over $2,000 in debt with no resources to pay. Robert knew he had sinned, and he repented before the Lord, begging mercy and a way out of trouble for the sake of his family as well as himself. The

Lord was merciful and more than kind. A few days before the expense accounting deadline, Robert was advised that his performance appraisal merited an increase in salary, and the company had decided to give it to him retroactively for a period of time. Did he want all of his money at once? Yes, and immediately. He was paid just in time to clear the credit card.

Robert shared his story with our prayer group. He literally wept for joy and praised God long and loudly for his goodness and mercy. However, by the end of the next year, Robert had slipped back into his old gears and once again brought himself to the brink of trouble with the inappropriate usage of his business credit card. Again, he humbled himself to the Lord, begging mercy. He made promises that he would never do this again. He had learned his lesson. The Lord again forgave him and orchestrated some unexpected revenue so that Robert could pay his debt and retain his job. Of course, our prayer group joined him in praise and thanksgiving.

Would you believe? He very shortly "forgot" to amend his ways, and of course, wound up in trouble at the end of the fiscal year for the third time! I'm sure the Lord heard all of the weeping and gnashing of teeth; but the answer was "no money this time." Robert was forced to confess his financial problems to his wife and then to secure a personal loan to be able to balance his business account. He and his family suffered a full year of payments. But Robert never misused the business card again.

The Lord had been merciful to say no, thereby forcing Robert into more self-discipline and financial responsibility. My friend had fallen into the habit of counting on the Lord to save him from the consequences of his own sin, even when he made little or no sincere effort to change. The Lord mercifully would not enable him to continue to err in his ways.

Sometimes circumstances are so critical that one has neither the time nor the ability to formulate even mentally the short prayer, "Lord, have mercy on me." These are the times that I utter the second of these two short prayers. I use the name of Jesus as a prayer. "Jesus! Jesus! Jesus!" It's truly amazing what can happen when a person simply yells out the name of Jesus as a plea for help.

Over and over I have been saved from the entanglement of automobile accidents. And, I have yelled for Jesus to save others from potential accidents I have witnessed. I'm talking about watching vehicles miss each other by a hair's breadth. The most dramatic of these incidents took place one evening when my daughter Laura and I were together driving in a snowstorm to a mountain retreat in New Hampshire. It was the evening rush hour on the interstate, and traffic was bumper to bumper on dangerously slick asphalt. We saw an oncoming car beginning to slide out of control into our traffic lane, and we both called out the name of Jesus. Within a few seconds about six cars veered, slammed on brakes, skidded, or spun off the road. We saw one car spin completely around before landing backwards into a snow bank. Not one car was dented! Not one person was hurt! Was this a coincidence? Of course not. It was Our Lord putting a little amazing grace into action. As soon as possible, we pulled out of traffic and spent a few minutes joining our hands and our hearts in prayers of praise and thanksgiving for the safe deliverance of all of those lives, including our own.

Another time I was driving alone on a heavily congested interstate in Connecticut when an 18-wheel truck freakishly lost a pair of wheels. They simply snapped off of his rear axle and rolled through the traffic to land a few yards in front of me. I could not change lanes or otherwise avoid the stack of wheels without crashing into another vehicle. I yelled, "Jesus!" The accident should have killed me. Instead, I walked away from a totally wrecked car with nothing more than jangled nerves and one magnificent bruise to remind me to be grateful for the life God has given to me.

On the Singing of Prayer

One year I beheld a dream come true when I was able to take voice lessons. My teacher was also a personal friend whom I had met in a prayer group. She had a beautiful classically trained soprano voice, which she had often used to the glory of God in church ministry. While we were chatting about choirs one day, she shared her feelings of being privileged to be able to sing as a form of prayerful worship.

When a person sings a hymn with a prayerful attitude towards God, something special happens. The body becomes engaged in prayer. The prayerful attitude has already brought the mind and spirit into communion with God, and the physical activity of singing has joined the body to mind and spirit. Therefore, the entire being of body, mind, and spirit becomes unified and uplifted to the Lord in an act of love. It means the ability to give of ourselves 100% to the worship of God. Indeed this is a pleasing sight unto the Lord.

Think about it. If we are 100% worshipping and God is 100% listening, then mighty things have got to be happening as the Holy Spirit moves upon us. How many times have you simply "felt better" after singing a hymn in church or after listening to the choir? How often has a dedicated and worshipful soloist left you feeling somehow uplifted or mercifully soothed despite all of your troubles?

None of this is contingent upon a person's ability to sing beautifully. It is the act of singing that is important, and if you can't sing, then pray out loud. Just use your body by using your voice. It doesn't matter how you sound to yourself or to others. Remember that it is a pleasing sound unto the Lord. And, it doesn't have to be confined to church activity.

Try singing to the Lord during the day, especially during your private prayer time. Praise him, thank him, and glorify him just for being a good God. Use any gospel songs, hymns, raps, or whatever inspirational music to which you have been exposed. The style doesn't matter, it's your heart that matters when you sing to the Lord. If you feel creative, make up your own little tunes. God loves them!

On the Dance of Prayer

Perhaps you are a person who better responds to music and the creative expression of yourself through dance. God loves that, too! Dancing before God as an act of praise and worship is found in the Old Testament.

> When the horses of Pharaoh with his chariots and his chariot drivers went into the sea, the Lord brought back the waters of the sea upon them; but the Israelites walked through the sea on dry ground.
>
> Then the prophet Miriam, Aaron's sister, took a tambourine in her hand; and all the women went out after her with tambourines and *with dancing*. And Miriam sang to them.
> "Sing to the Lord, for he has triumphed gloriously;
> horse and rider he has thrown into the sea."
> *Exodus 15:20-21 (NRSV)*

Miriam and the women were singing and dancing as they led the people in praise and thanksgiving to God for their deliverance from the Egyptians. And the dance of prayer was not confined to women. When he brought the ark of God to the city of David, the beloved King David also prayed in an explosion of dance:

> David *danced* before the Lord with all his might; David was girded with a linen ephod. So David and all the house of Israel brought up the ark of

the Lord with shouting, and with the sound of the trumpet.

II Samuel 6:14-15, (NRSV)

They must have truly made a loud and joyful noise unto the Lord that day; and they must have found dancing as a very natural manner in which to give love and glory to God.

If you are one of those people who cannot "carry a tune" or perhaps sounds more like a bull frog croaking than a human singing, you might discover a wonderful new world of prayer in dancing before the Lord. Using appropriate music in the background does help, but it is not really necessary. You can just carry the music in your mind or hum tunelessly as you focus upon loving and adoring the Lord. Then let your body begin to move in whatever motion or rhythm that seems to well up. Let the Holy Spirit be your instructor and lead you in dance movement pleasing unto the Lord.

On Conversational Prayer

Most of the time when I pray, I simply use conversational prayer. That is, I talk to God either silently in my mind or out loud. I don't use any format or formula. I chat with the Lord as I would with any other person present in my life. It is a very simple form of communication, and it is very intimate. I might be walking around the block, driving my car, washing dishes, or sitting in my living room. As a matter of fact, sometimes I consider some of these places, such as the spot before my kitchen sink, as holy ground because I have cumulatively spent so much time there praying and talking to the Lord.

I might be scrubbing pots, pausing to look out of my kitchen window. Sometimes there is a squirrel frolicking in the Canadian hemlock just outside the backdoor or mockingbirds fighting for local nesting territory. Whatever the season and whatever the scenery, it becomes a moment to praise God for his creation, for my home, for his blessings upon my family, and for loving me and being my God. I might just say something like, "Lord, thank you for sending that silly squirrel my way. He looks so ridiculous hanging from his toes, and I laugh at his antics. Through him, you have brought me another moment of joy which I appreciate very much."

There are some days in which my time spent on the holy spot before my kitchen sink is the only time I can find to talk to the Lord about my problems, to ask his guidance, or simply to seek his face as a comforting presence in my day.

"Lord, I'm not feeling too well today. And there is so much I have to do. I'm feeling a little overwhelmed. Please help me. Give me the strength and stamina to do my necessary household chores, to cook, to run errands and to be a supportive Mother today. Show me what I should do and what I should not do this day. I would like to just curl up in a warm cozy place and let the world go by. But I can't. Please carry me and let there be only one set of footsteps in the sand. I love you, Lord."

In Summary, the methods of prayer are as varied and distinctive as the people who pray. Corporate prayer simply means two or more persons praying the same prayer together. The most common example of corporate prayer is found in church worship where many people gather to pray together in liturgical or non-liturgical service. Prayer meetings, small groups, and every circumstance where people join together in prayer are instances of corporate prayer, even joining hands over a simple blessing of food at mealtime.

Individual prayer is that one-on-one experience of communication between a person and God. One good starting point to learning how to pray is to use prayers that have already been written by some of the renowned theologians of both past and present. Christian libraries and bookstores abound with devotional material, and formal prayer books have been around for centuries. Ask the Lord to help you find something that meets your needs.

Search the Bible for scripture that you can personalize to meet your prayer needs. The Word of God is the most direct path to praying in accord with the Holy Spirit when we seek the Lord. As you search the Bible, look to find the promises of God (his guarantees to be with you) and cling to them. Through time spent in the Word and the consequent spiritual growth experience, your faith grows along with your gift of prayer. In short time you might be amazed at your discoveries and the resulting changes in your life.

Singing and dancing before the Lord are joyous forms of prayer dating from the early events of the Old Testament. The body actively joins the mind and spirit for a total effort of giving oneself unto the Lord in prayer. At your next opportunity, browse through a hymnal and notice that many verses are either parallels to scripture or direct quotations. Singing these words affects your life, especially in the context of prayer and worship. If you are interested in dancing before the Lord, you may want to try this in private prayer to avoid disturbing the peace of congregational worship. However, some churches accept and even encourage dancing before the Lord. So join right in!

My very favorite method of prayer is simple conversation with the Lord. To "chat" with Jesus may seem downright irreverent to people already comfortable within their own prayer rituals. Nevertheless, this informal method of prayer produces freedom to speak from the heart in a simple and powerful manner at any time and under all circumstances.

Questions for Discussion:

1. Think upon the times you have spent in corporate prayer,

Beginning Methods of Prayer

either in church services or in small gatherings. Did you come away with any sense of unity with the other people and with Christ? Refer to Matt. 12:30 and 23:37 to see that Jesus wants us to be gathered together with him. Acts 2:42, 46-47 provides us with the example of the early Christians in corporate prayer.

2. Spend a few minutes browsing through the Psalms, and select one to personalize. Read it to the Lord. He will be pleased.

3. Start your own list of "guaranteed prayers" as you read contemplative works and scripture. Try Jeremiah 33:3 and Matthew 7:7-8.

4. Take the time to sing one song or hymn to the Lord each day. The sound of your voice is pleasing to the ear of God, no matter how you sound to yourself or those around you.

5. Remember the Lord loves to watch you dance before him, even if you have two left feet! Read Jeremiah 31:3-4.

6. If you are initially uncomfortable with conversational prayer, go into your mental prayer closet to practice. Read Matthew 6:6.

CHAPTER FIVE

Hearing from the Lord

Oh, Lord, I struggle so often to hear you. Many times I can't recognize your answer. My self-centered life raises walls against you. Please help me to smash those obstructions that I may understand and know your voice, especially now that I attempt to teach others how to listen. Amen.

Of course conversational prayer or any other prayer and communication with the Lord is not meant to be one-sided. He will answer us, but in order to understand him, we usually must learn to listen and to assimilate whatever the Lord is saying to us. It is called waiting upon the Lord. We "hear" from him in many ways—through Holy Scripture, by the events and circumstances of our life, through other people, often in our thought life, and sometimes by his still small voice.

Whatever we seem to understand as answers to prayer, it is never in conflict with the Bible or what we perceive as the written Word of God. Man may misinterpret or inaccurately communicate the Word, but within those scriptures lie the unalterable essence of spiritual truth that cannot be denied by those who love the Lord.

On the Study of Scripture

In providing us with the Word of God, the Bible becomes the most direct and concrete pathway to knowledge about God and can be used to affirm and validate whatever we perceive as answer to prayer. It is imperative—absolutely necessary—to study the scriptures with the commitment to learn the teachings of Our Lord. We cannot hope to walk in his footsteps or to understand his directives for our lives without both prayer and the study of his Word. Learning scripture becomes a life-changing experience through which Jesus becomes even more intimately connected to the soul. The discipline of frequent or daily Bible reading, studying with both method and focus, is necessary to develop the balance and spiritual knowledge to avoid the pitfalls of those false teachers and ungodly philosophers who thrive in our modern secular world.

There are several approaches to Bible study, all of which I have used at various points of my walk with the Lord. You can start with reading a book. I recommend choosing one of the gospels in the New Testament. Try the Book of John, which was written with the primary focus of the spiritual life of Jesus and his teachings. The gospels of Matthew and Luke focus more closely upon the historical aspects and the chronological events of the life of Jesus. Some people prefer to start with the Book of Mark, simply because it is the shortest of the four gospels. For a starting point in the Old Testament, I recommend the Book of Psalms, simply because I use the psalms as another basis for my prayer life. At any given point in my life and in any set of circumstances, I can always find a psalm to personalize for my prayer needs. The psalms never fail to bring me comfort, healing, and intimacy with the Lord.

Another wonderful method of studying the Word is by topic. For example, this book is a study on the topic of prayer. There are thousands of Christian books on the market in Christian bookstores, regular bookshops, and used book dealers. You can even browse through the web for resources. I do much of my shopping through *http://www.christianbook.com*, a Christian book distributor in Massachusetts.

Many of the study Bibles have included programs for reading through the Bible in a year. This isn't always starting from page 1 of the Book of Genesis through the final page of the Book of Revelation. Few people seem to get through the Bible this way. Instead, these programs guide the reader through selected readings from Genesis through Revelation, often with study notes, cross-references, and commentary to help the reader understand the life application of the written word. Many other study Bibles include study programs on topics like faith or living a Christian life. I have used these programs, both to study alone and with small groups; and I found the experience with others to be most enriching.

Whatever you decide is best for you, please run—don't walk—to a Bible to begin reading the Word of God. There you will find the Lord speaking to you, especially when you read with a prayerful attitude.

Knowledge of the Bible is most important when waiting on the Lord and listening for his answer to prayer, because those answers are most often found in the scriptures. The Holy Spirit will lead you to them and grant you the spiritual insight to apply the Word to your life. If you do not immediately understand, keep praying for divine guidance. His ways are of love and truth. He will never lead you into the errors of sin or any action displeasing to Himself.

On Events and Circumstances

Along with the majority of my Christian acquaintances, I believe that the most frequent way most of us understand the answer to prayer is through the events and circumstances of our lives.

I am reminded of the summer when I labored intensively

on a job search. By the grace of God, I had been able to return to college to complete a Bachelor of Science in Business, graduating exactly thirty years from my high school graduation. It had been a long hard struggle along the difficult road of night school, pursuing a life-long dream.

It was an exciting time for me as I labored over my resume, researched companies to match their employment needs with my job skills, and purchased the conservative clothes I needed to present the correct professional profile. The job market was especially tough that year, even for the very young graduates, much less us "more mature" candidates. There were so few jobs available that to receive an interview was a major accomplishment to be celebrated.

As much as I desired keenly to find exciting employment, I also wanted to be sure that I was following the Lord's plan. Therefore, whenever I completed an interview, I would pray that I not receive an offer for employment unless it was the path that the Lord had specifically chosen for me. Time after time I heard nothing from the company, even when the interviewer left me with high hopes for being hired. Sometimes, there was a better candidate to be chosen; sometimes the job opening was cancelled; or the position was combined with another one already established within the company. I began to feel disheartened and wondered what I was doing wrong. I guess I really didn't like the Lord closing all those doors in my face.

However, a few months later, my invalid mother was suddenly hospitalized with diabetic complications. Within the same week my father (also in ill health) suddenly collapsed with a threatened congestive heart failure triggered by the stress of mother's circumstances. Then both parents were hospitalized concurrently (at the same facility) with my father confined to the intensive care unit. I had to fly 1500 miles south to help care for my family for almost six weeks. My sister, brother, and I had to make some hard decisions and take the drastic action of admitting my mother to a nursing home for the rest of her life. Eight days later my father died in the hospital. By the time I returned home, I felt emotionally fragile, quite dysfunctional, and spiritually drained. It was several more weeks before I felt that I had returned to a somewhat normal life.

If I had been employed, I would have suffered even more stress, especially if I had to leave a new and very challenging position. The Lord had answered "no" to my prayers for employment, because he knew I needed to be available for an even greater task.

On the Lips of Others

Sometimes God speaks to me very simply and profoundly through another person as he did one beautiful Sunday morning when I arrived at church in a dither, to say the least. It was during those years of rearing very young children, when I attempted to be the perfect mother and to cope sensibly with all the confusion that seemed to reign constantly in our household. I was doomed to failure and depression had set in.

On that morning my two-year-old son had managed to spill or break everything he touched. His older sister had not fared much better. As a matter of fact, she had endured baby brother beyond the call of duty and was justifiably angry when her pretty clothes were accidentally messed up. The cat could not seem to decide to stay inside or outside; and as the children kept letting him in or out every few minutes, he was tracking fresh snow throughout the kitchen. The new puppy stubbornly ignored his latrine paper, preferring the comfort of our living room rug. Nevertheless, I somehow managed to dress, to slap on some makeup, and to haphazardly run a brush through my hair before packing children into coats, then into the car, and off to church services.

What was left of me rushed through church doors at least ten minutes after the service had started. My beloved friend

Jack, an usher that morning, quickly noted my distress and with tender concern asked me what had happened. As I poured out my tale of woe, his beautiful blue eyes seemed to understand, to care, and to comfort me. This handsome elderly gentleman just stood there with sunlight sparkling off his white mane of wisdom. Because he was apparently listening with much sympathy, I continued in self-pity to vent my misery. Suddenly he jerked me back to reality.

"Margaret, in ten years the dog and the cat will probably be dead and the children will be gone off to live their own lives. Then where will you be? Enjoy what you can in your life right now each day with those children and their animals and your home."

He was right!

I was suddenly ashamed of myself.

His advice sank deep. As I remembered the transitory nature of children growing up and the preciousness of each season of our lives, I raised my stooped shoulders and turned my head to another direction. I repented of my self-pity, and I felt grateful to have been disciplined in love. Through Jack's words, our Lord had crashed through my depression to remind me that my life is a wondrous gift to be enjoyed, not a burden to be endured.

On Our Thought Life

Answers to prayers are often perceived in our thought life. It might come as an inspiration, a sudden insight into understanding, a reminder of biblical teachings, a memory that connects somehow, or a seemingly strange unconnected thought that recurs and seems important. Sometimes, we just suddenly "know" the answer, and we cannot explain how or why, except by the grace of God. Many times the answer appears unclear, disturbing, or simply something we don't even want to think about. Nevertheless, it is an answer to prayer, and we must learn to pay attention. We often need to continue to pray for understanding until it is gained. God has much patience. He will continue to send his messages; He will not give up on us.

One part of our thought life is often labeled intuition. Like all gifts and skill sets, some people have more than others. Intuition is the ability to know something without a rational thought process, i.e. instant cognition. Intuitive knowledge may not have any identifiable rationale. To act upon it is an act of faith. I often describe it as being nudged or guided by the Holy Spirit.

Others might say, "Listen to yourself and follow your instincts." How often have you been told to trust your instincts? Instincts and intuitiveness walk hand in hand. They are deeply ingrained in each of us and impossible to logically explain. I encourage you to trust your intuitiveness. The sudden insight may be a gift from the Lord. Receive it. Prayerfully use it.

If you have little intuition or you cannot trust yourself to acknowledge what you inexplicably know, then you might avoid this path of communication with the Lord. It is not for everyone. However, you might decide to become more open to it and to explore a new dimension of your prayer life. Simply start by actively listening to yourself when you suddenly "know" something.

One Christmas season, two ladies of the church coordinated a project to raise funds and to purchase an assortment of personal items, food, and small gifts for baskets to be delivered by the Youth Group to the shut-ins and other very elderly members of our congregation. I knew they were having problems raising enough money, but I was shocked to hear they only had about one-third of the required funds only a week before the delivery deadline. Still, I did not want to intrude. I also did not like entertaining the thought of "sticking my hand out" to others at that time of year when "everybody" seems to be asking for money and when the common household is already beleaguered by the expenses of the season.

Nevertheless, I was nudged by the Holy Spirit. How? Well, I just couldn't let go of the thought that someone needed to tell the people at church on Sunday that the project was desperately underfunded. Someone needed to collect more money. Otherwise, the elderly and the shut-ins could be neglected, or at best given only a token gift. I thought about the situation; I prayed; and I squirmed in my seat.

Finally, I just knew that I had to stay after church and personally collect money for the project. God was gracious to help me overcome my reluctance to ask for money, and the people of my church were generous to quickly respond. I collected over $150, more than enough to meet the need. Our spiritual cup overflowed with blessing! We were able to add more names to the list. I later found out that no one else knew about the problem until I started asking for help.

On the Voice of the Lord

If we will be still and listen, the Lord will speak to us. In Biblical times, the Lord spoke audibly to some people, like Moses in the story of the burning bush (Exodus 3). When Jesus was baptized by John the Baptist, the Lord spoke to the crowd, saying, "This is my Son, whom I love, with him I am well pleased." (Matt. 3:17, NIV) In both instances, the people heard the Lord's voice through their external ears. This rarely happens today.

Even so, I remember being in a terrible dilemma one time. Through a complicated and confusing series of events, I arrived at a point of feeling misunderstood and abandoned by several friends. Unfortunately, there was no possible way for me to defend myself without revealing highly confidential, very personal, and destructive information about other people. I was bursting with anger, hurt, and distress. Then I began to tell the Lord about it. Even though I knew he was

Hearing from the Lord

aware of all the circumstances of my life, I needed to ventilate my emotions.

This intensive mental conversation with Jesus occurred while I was unloading a car full of groceries. I finished my story by saying, "Lord, they just don't understand!"

"I understand."

I almost dropped my groceries I was so startled.

That soft voice seemed to have come from over my right shoulder; and I turned around, looking around to see who was speaking to me.

No one was standing there.

I clung to my arms full of groceries with my jaw hanging open. The stunning realization hit me that the Lord had spoken. I had heard His voice aloud! The horrible tension shattered within me. Pain crumbled in my gratitude of being understood and comforted by the only person who really counted. Jesus, Jesus, precious Jesus! Tears of joyful relief flowed. I had been touched by Divine Love in a life-changing moment.

Since that event, I have realized that most of the time, most of us hear from the Lord in a still, quiet voice heard only by ourselves. Amazingly, you can come to recognize the voice of the Lord as Jesus, himself, taught in the parable of the good shepherd:

> The man who enters by the gate is the shepherd of his sheep. The watchman opens the gate for him, and the sheep listen to his voice. He calls his own sheep by name and leads them out. When he has brought out all his own, he goes on ahead of them, and his sheep follow him because they know his voice. But they will never follow a stranger... because they do not recognize a stranger's voice.
>
> I am the good shepherd; I know my sheep and my

sheep know me—just as the Father knows me and I know the Father—and I lay down my life for the sheep. I have other sheep that are not of this sheep pen. I must bring them also. They too will listen to my voice, and there shall be one flock and one shepherd.

John 20:2-4, 14-16 (NIV)

Just as Jesus is the good shepherd, we are the sheep of his pasture who come to know His voice as we follow Him. The key to hearing His voice is to practice listening. Pray to the Lord and then sit quietly listening for several minutes. Listen proactively—that is, with a conscious effort to expel all distractions—to seek Him within your quiet inner self. You might find that you have not heard the Lord previously, simply because you have not waited and listened with an expectant heart. Learning to hear the Lord is a life-long experience, so do not be dismayed at the outset. He will come and speak to you. Just be still and listen.

On Bible Browsing

One morning I grabbed my Bible and a hot cup of coffee. Then I returned to bed to snuggle down into my blankets and to have a morning chat with the Lord. Although I felt an urgency to return to the work of this composition, I felt less than confident of performing the task. So I very simply asked Jesus for inspiration, hoping for a special "word" regarding this book. Carefully, I began to Bible browse, that is, to randomly open to a page several times, scanning each page until some of the words seem to leap up at me. One of my friends calls this methodology the "lucky dip" method. Others believe it is a "horrible" practice. I know it only as a position of listening to whatever the Lord wants to tell me—an attitude of hearing without imposing my own agenda. Sometimes what I "hear" through the scriptures apparently relates to whatever is on my heart at that time. But often, it does not. Those times seem to be the Lord taking advantage of having gained my attention to tell me something far more important. Although you may laugh, I have found it to be a useful avenue of amazing grace too often to be a coincidence. "Ask and ye shall receive...." And, receive, I did. I noted the verses and phrases that seemed to be important to me at that moment. Then I copied them sequentially to compose God's response.

1. A bad messenger plunges men into trouble, but a faithful envoy brings healing. (Proverbs 13:17, RSV)

2. As you do not know how the spirit comes to the bones in the womb of a woman with child, so you do not know the work of God who makes everything. (Ecclesiastes 11:5 - RSV)

3. ...Break up your fallow ground, and sow not among thorns. (Jeremiah 4:3, RSV)

4. For the earth will be filled with the knowledge of the glory of the Lord, as the waters cover the sea. (Habakkuk 2:14, RSV)

The first verse I received as a warning. Very realistically, I am just a messenger struggling to transmit thoughts, teachings, and inspirations I have received from the Lord. The Lord is cautioning me to report what I receive without embellishments and to be a faithful envoy capable of bringing his healing through his words. He does not want any confusion or trouble due to my embroidered accounts of storytelling.

I laughed when I read the second verse. It was loud and clear: "You'll never be able to figure it out!" How many times have I spent enormous amounts of energy trying to understand my sovereign God. What a waste of time! I think myself inside out, upside, downside, and roundside, when I should realize the most profound wisdom of man is but foolishness compared to the mind of God. Actually it is an extraordinary relief to understand that I can't understand, nor do I need to understand, what this is all about. It takes a huge load off of my mind to let the Lord be responsible for the job.

The third portion of this message seems short and sweet, but it revealed many layers to me. Obviously I am not to waste time and energy sowing my seeds among the thorns. What thorns? Who? When I casually opened my Bible the next evening, I landed in chapter eight of the Book of Luke in the middle of the parable of the sower. Consider what happened to some of the seed.

> And some fell among thorns; and the thorns grew with it and choked it. And some fell into good soil and grew, and yielded a hundred fold. (Verses 7 and 8a)

A little later Jesus explains the parable.

> And as for what fell among the thorns, they are those who hear, but as they go on their way they are choked by the cares and riches and pleasures of life, and their fruit does not mature. And as for that in the good soil, they are those who, hearing the word, hold it fast in an honest and good heart, and bring forth fruit with patience. (Verses 14 and 15)

Well, my mind relegates pagans, unbelievers, and cultural Christians into the category of seed abiding with thorns. I use the term "cultural Christians" to describe people who visit church for the purpose of social gathering, especially upon occasions like baptisms and marriages. They have an ingrained belief that there really is a God, to whom they pray during emergencies. However, they shy away from the concept of Jesus as Lord of their lives, often claiming they do not particularly care about religion—that is, until their deathbed is in sight. I fear this book and its seed may not interest those cultural Christians, although I would love to attract their attention.

What about breaking up the fallow ground for seeding? Fallow ground is land that has been plowed, but not seeded for a season or more, often to destroy weeds or otherwise improve the soil. The soil must be good earth capable of nurturing a bountiful harvest or the farmer would not invest such a great deal of time and work behind the plow. Figuratively speaking, fallow ground means uncultivated or inactive. The idea of the complacent Christian comes to my mind. I am referring to people who finally understand and accept the salvation of Jesus Christ, then settle themselves into a comfortable spiritual standstill. They delightfully rest in the grace and mercy of their deliverance from sin without thought to placing their lamps upon a stand to shine against the darkness. The complacent Christian endeavors to perpetuate a state of "happiness is knowing Jesus" without ever attempting to help others out of their spiritual pits. After all, that might prove to be inconvenient or even downright uncomfortable!

Consequently my thought of breaking up the fallow ground is the notion of stirring these people with new approaches to prayer and spiritual communion with God. My prayer is that this book might in some small way prepare their minds and spirits to hear the Lord and to receive his word as seed, so that they can sow and reap a bountiful spiritual harvest.

> Sow for yourselves righteousness,
>   reap the fruit of steadfast love;
> break up your fallow ground,

> for it is time to seek the Lord,
> that he may come and rain salvation upon you.
> *Hosea 10:12 (RSV)*

It is also my prayer that new Christians—the babes in Christ—may find comfortable and appropriate methods of prayer among these pages. And, I hope that many others find an enhancement to their prayer lives as they explore some of the paths of communication with God described briefly in the following pages.

As I try to envision a bountiful harvest of steadfast love springing from the rain of salvation, I look forward to the final part of my little conversation with the Lord. It is the promise of Habakkuk that...the earth (these people of God) will be filled with the knowledge of the glory of the Lord.... It is the promise of mind boggling and incomprehensible wonders, as much knowledge as the waters that the cover the sea. This is just too much for me to receive. I feel overwhelmed. I can't begin to understand but a tiny portion of the knowledge of God. However, I do know that it begins with prayer, that is, both the giving and the receiving of communication with our Lord.

In Summary, we hear from the Lord in many ways in answers to our prayers. Most Christians will acknowledge they can hear from the Lord through his holy word, the Bible. Certainly, the study of scripture is the most important link in understanding God and what he would say to us. Perhaps the second most common understanding of God's answer to our prayers is through the events and circumstances arising after we have sought the Lord. Often we can hear him simply through conversations with others, friends, teachers, and pastors. Our thought life frequently can be the conduit of God's message. We must learn to listen to our own thoughts and to determine if they are from above. The voice of the Lord is available to us today, even as throughout the ages. Be still and listen for his gentle whisperings, the small still voice from within. The more adventurous may want to browse through the Bible looking for scriptures that seem to leap from the page. However you choose to seek the Lord in prayer, he will answer you. Listen and wait.

Questions for Discussion:

1. Read Eccl 2:22-25. Think about it and read it again. Now pray for understanding of what the Lord is telling you. If you are comfortable, share this with someone.

2. Have you ever seen your answer to prayer in an event or set of circumstances? If so, how did the Lord change things? Did you realize at the time, that this was the answer to your prayer?

3. Have you ever experienced hearing from the Lord through others? Perhaps you thought it was a coincidence. In the world of prayer, it is called a "God-incidence!"

4. Take note of your thought life. Is there something you keep thinking about? Ask the Lord if he is trying to talk to you.

5. In 1 Kings:12, Job 4:12 & 16, you will find both Elijah and Job hearing the voice of the Lord in stillness and quiet. Discuss this possibility in your own life, and take time to practice listening. The Lord still speaks to individuals everyday!

6. If you like the idea, try to browse through the Bible and pick out 2 or 3 scriptures that seem to "leap" from the page. Write them out, study them, and see if they apply

to your life today. Although this method is not for everyone, you may find yourself unexpectedly delighted.

CHAPTER SIX

Praying Beyond Words

Lord, as we behold the wonders of creation, as we become more aware of your loving mercy, as we learn to sense your presence more acutely in our lives, please help us to become more vulnerable and open to spiritual growth by your amazing grace. Thank you.

When I was a very little girl, I thought that I could only pray when I was kneeling down with my hands clasped together in a certain way and my head bowed down. This was done best in church, but could also be accomplished at home, for example, by my bedside. Even as I grew in age and spiritual development, I was confined by form and format in learning how to pray. Perhaps my greatest hindrance was simply words. I could not always find the words to pray. Either I could not find them in written form or I could not find them within myself. Despite the passage of years and the development of my prayer life along all of the lines discussed in the previous chapters, I still found a communication gap in my prayers. It was on my side of the prayer, not God's. I needed to discover ways to pray beyond words, because words could not always convey what I was feeling inside. I also realized that sometimes words could limit whatever the Lord was telling me.

On Joy

During communion at church, I commonly experience the prayer of joy. I usually await my turn with a sense of anticipation for a wondrous gift. Sometimes I even get a little nervous and my heart beats a littler faster than normal. I receive the bread and wine with a childlike joy and wonder. I cannot explain what happens to me. I just know that the Lord has come to me in a very special way. He has touched me intimately. I feel a little more healed and whole as a person. Often I want to volcanically erupt, splashing some of my joy all over everyone in sight. It is Divine Joy. I can't hold on to it and keep it to myself. This happiness has to be shared.

At other times, the joy comes in a different form. It reaches into the inner depths of my being and instills a strength which feeds my spirit. It is a different form of Divine Joy, more quiet and serene. Nevertheless it also must be shared, for hoarding the Lord's love in any form simply will not work.

The joy which I find easiest to share is laughter—a chuckle, a giggle, or even raucous laughter until the tears flow. This may seem irreverent to many folks, but it happens. The Lord has a sense of humor, finely honed and attuned to each individual. He will cause circumstances and event to make us laugh. Look for them!

On Gratitude

At times I feel so absolutely overwhelmed by the love of my God that I lift my heart and spirit in a prayer of gratitude. Words cannot express my thoughts and feelings of the moment. For example, when I look upon the gift of my children, I am grateful to God beyond words. A long list of "thank you's" cannot begin to express my love and appreciation for all I have been given in my life.

Whenever I stop to consider this earth and the physical

existence of life, I find it mind-boggling. Think about it the next time you view the grandeur of mountains or seashore or even a simple raindrop. Creation is simply too awesome to be articulately described in prayer. Impossible! So, how do I thank God for all of creation, even a tiny part of it? With a fervent attitude of gratitude for his divine love—a prayer beyond words.

On Imaging

A few years ago, I discovered the use of my imagination as a tool of prayer. That is, I learned to use mental images to project complete thoughts to the Lord. This makes use of the old adage that a picture is worth a thousand words. It also fully covers me in some areas where I really don't know how to pray otherwise.

I find my inspirations for imaging in many places. Most notably I have been using mental pictures of posters that I have seen in Christian bookstores, homes, and other places. One of my favorites is the picture of a shirt with the focus on the pocket located over the man's heart. Tucked inside of the pocket is a fluffy, tiny, baby duckling, buttoned securely to keep it held safely in place. I often hold this in my mind when I am praying for someone who might feel endangered, emotionally fragile, or in grief. Since I don't always know what will bring comfort to a person, I feel somewhat helpless in trying to pray very specifically. So, I simply ask Jesus to hold that person close to his heart. Then I continue to envision that person and the poster image as a thought package of prayer whenever I might think to do so. It is also a simple, quick, and very direct method, which I use frequently when I am finding it difficult to put aside sufficient time to pray more at length.

When I pray for the Lord to bring joy into a person's life, I might imagine another poster. The picture is of a child delightedly romping through a field on a sunny day with flowers, bluebirds, butterflies, and green grass in abundance. The caption reads, "Lord, you thought of everything!" The child appears totally happy and wanting for nothing. So, I picture the person for whom I am praying and the image of the poster as I ask the Lord to bring the child within that person to a place of joy where he might unabashedly delight in all that he beholds. Again and again I will envision those images and project them to the Lord as a repetitive prayer.

Although posters and pictures are useful starting points, the resources for prayer images are only limited by our imagination. If I think of a child having trouble earning good grades in school, I might pray for him simply by envisioning him returning home just beaming with joy as he proudly displays a good test score or an excellent report card. I might pray for a bountiful harvest by imagining my garden laden with ripe vegetables to be picked. The possibilities are never ending.

On Dreams

When I approach the subject of dreams as a method of communication with God, I am not referring to the definition of "dreaming" as a purposeful thought process or as an imaginative creation. I am addressing the dreams that we receive in the process of going to sleep or awakening from sleep.

The mental self in each of us is psychologically composed of both the conscious and the subconscious (often referred to as the unconscious). Dreaming is a mental activity arising from the subconscious. The individual has very little control over it. Also, the subconscious cannot lie, i.e. it is the truest part of the person, free from self-inflicted untruths and the intentionally bent versions of personal reality. Because of this, the subconscious becomes another communication channel for the Lord to use in communing with us.

This is not a new concept. Both the Old Testament and the New Testament of the Bible are filled with dreams and their interpretation. Some examples include Jacob's ladder, King Nebuchadnezzar's dream with Daniel's interpretation, and Joseph's warning to flee with Mary and Baby Jesus to the safety of Egypt. Historically, dreams and visions have carried great weight in the affairs of mankind, especially within the confines of religion and spiritual insight.

Rest assured there are piles of books written on the subject for the reader to pursue. These not only include historical accounts, but modern day theological and psychological studies. However, it is my intent to only lightly touch upon the subject as another method of prayer.

One critical element of dream life is the use of symbols. Seldom will a dream be a picture of daytime thought-conscious representations. And, the understanding of the symbolical is unique to the dreamer. It is usually impossible for the dream to be fully understood by another person. However, there appear to be some patterns of symbols common to most people, and a competent psychologist can often help the person to explore the meaning of his or her dreams and to learn how to interpret his or her own personal dream language.

There is another important truth to be mentioned here. *Sound theology and sound psychology walk hand in hand.* There is no conflict. The Bible promotes mental health along with spiritual health. The Lord heals and guides us through dreams today as well as he did two thousand years ago.

A couple of years ago, I found myself overburdened with anger. Some of this anger I could understand from the personal circumstances of that period of my life. However, I finally realized that I was overreacting to many things, and that I was laboring under a monumental load of undefined anger. I finally admitted that I could not solve my problem alone, and I decided to seek help before I found myself in a terrible crisis. I enlisted the aid of two people, a psychologist and a priest. The psychologist had to be open to understanding and to working with my spiritual life, and the priest had to be equally accepting of the concept of psychological healing. I felt that I could not proceed "in balance" without both resources.

Shortly thereafter, I had a remarkable dream. I was driving a car, and as I turned the car towards the garage, the door opened automatically. The garage was separate and apart from the house. Also the garage was filled with assorted household furnishings, including a rectangular table standing in the middle and in the front of everything. A black female cat was comfortably curled up on top of the table. The cat was sleek, beautiful, and healthy. She simply took notice of my glaring headlights, casually arose, and walked away. End of dream.

Interpretation of the dream came in bits and pieces and over a period of weeks. I realized that all of the elements of the dream represented parts of my subconscious self. The image of my driving the car represented my conscious control of self as I purposed myself to get help to discover my problems and their solutions. The garage represented my past as separate from the house of my present (life). The furnishings being stored there were symbols of old memories not a part of my present life. The sleeping cat represented my subconscious self to be revealed in the light of revelation and therapy.

In my mind there were two noteworthy aspects of the cat: (1) She was not startled by the headlights! A real cat would have freaked out and streaked away in a panic. She simply moved over to let me in. (2) She was a lovely specimen of a cat with nothing to mar her beauty. I was amazed when I discovered her to symbolize something beautiful inside of me. A part of me! Within the view of my own lousy self-image, I had never considered myself to be beautiful in any way. All in all, I found the dream to be an affirmation of the direction I had taken, as well as a sign of hope and comfort that I needed. I felt it was a gift from the Lord, and I praised and thanked him for it.

On Visions

We can receive visions from the Lord in the same manner we receive dreams through the subconscious. The primary difference between the dream and the vision is that the vision is received while a person is wide-awake, often with eyes open. The vision is not created from the person's imagination or in any other manner voluntarily constructed. It is always received. And again, this is not new, at least from a biblical perspective. The Book of Revelation is saturated with visions.

It is important to note that some people will never receive a vision in their entire lives. Others will find it common. These are spiritual gifts and mysteries of the Lord, which I do not attempt to justify, defend, or completely understand. The visions I have received usually have occurred during or shortly after time spent in prayer, often in a prayer group or in a church service. The first time it happened to me, I simply did not understand what was going on!

I had joined three friends to attend a meeting of the Order of St. Luke, a ministry sanctioned by the Episcopal Church and focused upon prayer for healing the sick. After the meeting, we adjourned to the church for a Eucharist service. As the priest moved through his prayers, I observed a light blink on for a few seconds over his head. I thought my eyes were playing tricks on me, so I rubbed them several times. But the light appeared again and again. It was shaped like a golden balloon and rested just for a second or two on the head of the priest. I looked around and found the same thing happening to other people who were immersed in deep prayer. This experience lasted for at least ten minutes.

After the service I described the lights to one of my companions, and asked her if she had ever experienced such a sight. No, but she hazarded a guess that it might have been the aura of the Holy Spirit. I remained confused. Later I realized that what I had seen was somewhat similar to the golden halos that are painted on many icons and other holy pictures. I wondered if those artists had also seen the lights. When I was finally able to describe this event to the priest, he was utterly amazed. He believed what I told him, and he felt blessed. All I could understand was that I had been uniquely blessed to witness a spiritual movement among the people of God.

Most of the time I receive visions in answer to prayer or as an extended part of prayer, and my eyes are usually closed. Not long ago, I was praying with a group focusing upon my friend Mary. We asked the Lord to heal the abused and neglected child within Mary so that she could become a more whole and healthy adult. I had completed my petition, and I still had my eyes closed. Suddenly, in my mind's eye, I could see Mary as a little girl in a pretty dress, ribbon in her hair, and holding a big lollipop in one hand with a doll in the other hand. Jesus walked over to her, knelt down to her height, and talked to her. Then they both sat on the ground together and began to play a game. End of vision.

When I described the vision to her, Mary shared several things about it that were very important to her. First of all, she grew up in very poor circumstances with never enough food in the house, much less a big lollipop. All of the children in her family were clothed from the church's donations of second-hand clothes, which were seldom very pretty or fit very well. She had no doll until she was eleven years old. And, as the youngest of seven children, Mary never felt she had playmates interested in the games she wanted to play. She always had to tag along with older siblings and play their games if she wanted company. Therefore, Mary found my vision a very comforting and loving experience. Together we praised the Lord and thanked Him.

On Personal Offerings and Sacrifices

Doing things such as collecting money, can sometimes be

Praying Beyond Words

distasteful. However, when we can offer up these actions as a personal sacrifice to the Lord, it becomes another form of prayer—a very active form of prayer.

When I was a little girl, the Roman Catholic nuns taught me to make personal offerings as sacrifices to God. I was encouraged to use the offering as an intercessory prayer for someone. I can remember struggling in my child's world to connect this sacrifice to doing homework, cleaning up my room, or taking care of my brother and sister. I would pray to God to let Him know that I was offering him this sacrifice because I was not too happy about any of it. These prayers sometimes helped me to get through the difficult moments of my young life. Actually, I began to realize that if I could not get out of the unpleasantness, I could at least make good use of it.

Even today, in my adult world, this still applies. I am glad to be reminded of it because there are countless tasks I must accomplish that are thankless, distasteful, or unrewarding. These are simply things I must do (like housekeeping), and I have to accomplish them because I am responsible. If I could remember to dedicate these tasks as offerings of prayer, I could experience a life changing spiritual movement in my life. It was so in my childhood, perhaps it can be so again—beginning now. I can do it by taking the hand of Jesus and walking through the task with Him. Using these personal offerings as extended intercessory prayer, the task then becomes holy and my attitude changes.

The prayer of sacrifice can be extended to include many things, especially pain and suffering beyond our control. The martyrdom of the saints and the innocents of early Christianity are a most dramatic example. Although few of us may have occasion to offer martyrdom to the Lord, many of us have daily physical and emotional pain to offer up to the Lord as prayer. I am not recommending that anyone delay the healing of pain in order to make a sacrifice, but I am suggesting that the pain we must suffer can be brought to the altar of our Lord as a prayer.

Perhaps the personal sacrifice of fasting is the most common form of *prayer beyond words* practiced throughout the Christian church. Today the liturgical churches still require some fasting during the penitential seasons of Lent and Advent. In many of churches, it is common procedure for people to fast as a preparation for communion, ordination, and other sacraments or spiritual ordinances. Sometimes the whole congregation might be requested to fast and pray for a special need. The traditions vary. However, fasting is certainly a very old practice, and it is found in both the Old and the New Testaments.

During Old Testament times, fasting was most often extreme, taken to the point of gauntness, and combined with the wearing of sackcloth and ashes, such as depicted with Job in grief over the loss of his family and possessions (Job 16:18, NIV). In several of the psalms, King David speaks of humbling himself before the Lord with prayer, fasting, and the wearing of sackcloth and ashes as he prayed for people who were ill (Ps. 35:13; 69:10-11; 109:24, NIV). Other Old Testament stories depict God's people fasting and praying for guidance, deliverance from evil, and even national repentance. Today, we leave the external signs of sackcloth and ashes behind because Jesus taught that proper fasting is done in secret, not obvious to men, but only to our heavenly Father (Matt. 6:16-18, NIV).

Within the New Testament, it is important to note that Jesus himself fasted immediately after being baptized by John in preparation for his ministry.

> Jesus, full of the Holy Spirit, returned from the Jordan and was led by the Spirit in the desert, where for forty days he was tempted by the devil. He ate nothing during those days, and at the end

of them he was hungry.

Luke:4:1-2 (NIV)

Later in the New Testament, the Book of Acts refers to the prophets and teachers in the church at Antioch worshipping the Lord and fasting. Then they laid hands on Paul and Barnabus before sending them off on a missionary journey (Acts 13:1-3, NIV). As they formed new churches, "Paul and Barnabus appointed elders for them in each church and, with prayer and fasting, committed them to the Lord, in whom they had put their trust" (Acts 14:23, NIV).

Although many people throughout the ages have found powerful prayer experiences while fasting, my own experience is somewhat limited. During my childhood years the Roman Catholic Church required me to fast before receiving communion, and I remember being very anxious about forgetting and taking a few sips of water when I brushed my teeth. Since I also have the tendency to become dizzy and even to faint when I am fasting, my early experiences left me with a sour note to overcome later in life. However, during my walk as a Protestant Christian, I have encountered fasting, not as a requirement, but as a request by a church or a group of people who have committed themselves to prayer and fasting for a specific reason. And, I have found this to be a much more fruitful and fulfilling spiritual walk.

Fasting can be accomplished on very many levels, from eating and drinking nothing (including water) to only abstaining from certain foods. Each person who wants to fast must determine his own guidelines. Most of the time I refrain from solid foods, but I do drink some nourishing liquids because this works best for me. When do I fast? Only when the Holy Spirit leads me to do so! If someone asks me to join in prayer and fasting for their own reasons, I try to answer that I will ask the Lord if this is something he wants me to do. When the Lords wants me to fast, I can do so without fear of dizziness or any other problems because I then have his grace and mercy to proceed with the task.

On Vicarious Suffering

There is another type of personal suffering that becomes a dimension of prayer. It is described as vicarious suffering, that is, suffering another's pain. For me, this experience has mostly been in the area of grief.

I remember when a friend experienced tragedy. Her grown son was badly injured in a freak sled accident while on vacation. He was hospitalized in critical condition and spent about ten days in and out of intensive care, including two surgical procedures, before he finally died. For many months, every time I thought of her and her family, I felt a crushing sadness, an internal physical ache, and the grief of a mother for her lost child. I was grieving for her, not for myself. When I recognized this as vicarious suffering, I offered it to the Lord as a prayer to help her to survive the overwhelming burden of grief.

Remember that sometimes the Lord calls us to help carry another person's heartache.

On the Peace of the Lord

Just as we can carry/receive another person's pain, so can we receive another person's peace and love. Also, we can carry this peace and love as a gift to others. Have you ever seen another person who has the capacity to bring peace and serenity into the most chaotic, miserable and unhappy circumstances? I think of Corrie ten Boom and her sister, who brought compassion, mercy and love to the inmates of their concentration camp in World War II. They ministered the peace of the Lord amid the most inhuman circumstances of cruelty and suffering.

We daily walk through trials and tribulations all around us, although this may not be on the level of a world war. Nevertheless, all around us are circumstances of people desperately in need of peace. My friend Mary has this gift of ministry, and she uses it prayerfully. She simply centers herself upon the Lord, receives his peace and carries it to others in adversity.

> Peace I leave with you; my peace I give to you. I do not give to you as the world gives. Do not let your hearts be troubled, and do not let them be afraid.
>
> *John 14:27 (NRSV)*

Mary reaches out in love and stills the storms of life around her. She ministers the peace of the Lord. I chuckle as I almost find myself waiting to see her walk on water through the power of Jesus!

In Summary, I thank the Lord for giving us many ways to pray beyond the limitations of words. We can commune with the Lord through our emotions, especially joy and gratitude. We can return his divine love with our own human love, totally acceptable and pleasing to Him.

Using images is a creative way to communicate with the Lord. Avoid frustration when you simply can't articulate your prayer. Lack of words cannot stop you from beaming your thoughts to our Lord, who receives your heartfelt intent with clear understanding.

The Lord has been speaking to his people in dreams and visions since time immemorial. Dreams and visions are also a prayer, when defined as a communication from the Lord, especially in the area of prophecy. It is important to pray for clear understanding because the message is often couched in symbolical movement.

Personal sacrifice unto the Lord offers us endless means of prayer. More importantly, this sacrificial prayer transforms us and changes our lousy attitudes. We move from grumbling to gratitude for the opportunity to draw closer to Jesus. Whether it is work, pain, or fasting, these sacrifices are a true labor of love, holy and pleasing unto the Lord.

The vicarious suffering for others is a gift of prayer, especially for intercessory prayer warriors. It is a means by which the Holy Spirit guides us to pray and spiritually releases us when the job is done.

Communion with the Lord often brings us "the peace which passes understanding." It is not only his answer to our prayer, but it is a gift which he enables us sometimes to pass onto others.

Questions for Discussion:

1. Can you identify a moment in which you were aware of deep joy or gratitude connected with the presence of God in your life? Read 1Thess 5:16.

2. Think of a situation or problem in which you might find difficulty to express prayer in words. Ask the Holy Spirit to help you create an image in your mind, which can reflect your heart, and offer it as a prayer to the Lord

3. Discuss a dream you have had and the consequences it made in your life. Can you look at the dream as a message from the Lord? See Gen 40:8b.

4. Many people are reluctant to acknowledge visions. Refer to Numbers 12:6 for God's word on visions, and then read Acts 10:9-19 as a New Testament example. If possible, share a vision with the group.

5. The next time you have to do something you find unpleasant, try offering it to the Lord as a sacrifice of intercession for someone who needs prayer.

Praying Beyond Words

6. Have you ever fasted by yourself or with a group? How did the experience affect you? Refer to 2 Chron 20:3 and Esther 4:15-16 for more Biblical examples.

7. Vicarious suffering is another form of prayer initiated by the Holy Spirit calling upon specific people for specific intercession. Be aware of the possibility and be willing to pray.

8. Read John 14:27 again, as well as John 16:33. End the study session by asking the Lord for his peace and the opportunity to share it with others.

CHAPTER SEVEN

Christian Mysticism

Lord, how can I explain the unexplainable? I can't. So, please help me to share in words a part of those small mystical encounters with you. Guide and direct my thoughts and my pen. Thank you.

When he read the outline of *Break Ground*, Pastor Enoch announced, "I see something here that disturbs me."

"What?" I asked.

"It's this word *mysticism*."

"Well, don't you believe in dreams and visions from the Lord? How about the word of knowledge and the spiritual gift of discernment?" I asked.

"Yes, I know these things to be true and sent from God."

"Were these things logical, that is, 'man-minded'? Weren't they subject to human rationale?"

"No."

"Then they were spiritual versus logical. They were the mystical experiences of communion with God, who is mysterious, often puzzling, and beyond our comprehension. And, what about the mystical body of Christ—his people here on earth?"

"OK, I'll think about that."

When I approach the subject of mysticism, I am strictly

defining mysticism within the realm of the Judeo-Christian experience. I am not, and have never been, subjected to the eastern forms or mystical rites of the non-Christian. My mystical experiences are related only to the triune godhead of Father, Son and Holy Spirit. These are faith experiences, not to be confused with psychological phenomena or occult practices. I cannot "conjure" them up. However, I can choose to reject them or to receive them just as I can choose to accept or reject any other gift in life.

Mystical experiences are very subjective and usually distinctive to each person. That makes sense because each mind is an entity unto its own, and not able to be duplicated, just as each person's relationship to God is distinctive and largely unparalleled by another. This is all part of the mystery of our beloved God. The mystical experience deals with realities beyond intellectual understanding. It is a form of communion with God which is sometimes difficult to perceive and impossible to understand. Yet these things do happen, especially to those who are open to them.

The Christmas following the death of my father was a particularly difficult time for me although I had no problem dealing with the theological aspect of the season. As always, I was grateful for the birth of Christ, my own personal Messiah, and I loved the celebration of his coming to earth. However, I suffered from resurrected memories of the past regarding the alcoholic behavior of my father during the Christmas seasons of my childhood. In fact, I can never remember my father being sober during Christmas. He was always drunk on Christmas Eve and "hung over" on Christmas morning. Therefore, my joy of giving and receiving gifts was always tarnished by his condition. On the season following his death, every time I thought of Christmas, I would see in my "mind's eye" a picture of my drunken Daddy sitting at the base of the Christmas tree distributing gifts. I found myself unable to approach even the thought of the Yuletide season without distress. I could not think about gift giving, much less shopping for presents. Nor could I approach sending out seasonal greetings. I could enjoy our little nativity crèche, some poinsettias, and even a wreath on the door, but I could not desire a tree in my home, nor could I look forward to the exchange of gifts. However, I had no problem preparing food and eagerly anticipating our holiday feast with the family, perhaps because times of festival usually include special foods and meals with family. Altogether, I was feeling quite torn up inside.

About this time, my daughter Laura reminded me that I should try hard not to ruin Christmas for the rest of the family, even though I was still suffering. She was right. So, I asked her to shop with me for my gift to my husband. I had delegated all the other shopping chores to him, but I could not ask him to buy his own gift. She agreed, and we went together on a shopping expedition. As I was walking through one of the stores, I happened to pass a display of artificial Christmas trees. Although I wanted to rush pass them, I suddenly felt "stopped in my tracks" by a strong spiritual movement as I approached a certain tree decorated with old-fashioned ornaments. At the base of the tree was a music system with small speakers emitting Christmas carols. There was something important about that spot, and I stood rooted there for several minutes although I felt very uncomfortable about looking at the tree. Eventually I moved along, only to return again and again to that very same spot. I began to feel like I was a little girl again. By the third time I returned to the tree, I felt like I was standing on holy ground and someone was holding my hand. But, I still felt uncomfortable about looking at the Christmas tree.

When we returned to her apartment, I described to Laura what had happened to me. As I talked to her I had a sudden revelation. I knew what had happened. Jesus had taken my hand and made me look at the Christmas tree. He was literally walking by my side through this painful time, and he was letting me know I would be all right. With Jesus by my side, I could look at the family traditions of Christmas again. He had comforted me and brought me tremendous healing. I praised and thanked the Lord!

My experience at the Christmas tree was an unsolicited and unannounced visit from on high, a truly mystical experience. I really had no control over it, except for one very important aspect. I could have ignored or rejected the mystical presence. After all, Our Lord does not force his love on us.

On Meditation

In Chapter Five, I discussed the study of scripture as one means of hearing from the Lord. When we study and think upon the Bible, we are in fact "meditating upon the Word." However, there are other forms of prayerful meditation to draw closer to God. We can meditate upon His presence in our lives—not what He says or does, but His spiritual, almost physical nearness.

Meditation is the path one can intentionally follow which often leads to mystical experience. I first encountered meditation in an ecumenical group of Christian women. At the time I did not know that it was a form of meditation; I only recognized it as a new (to me) and unusual method of praying. The lady who led the worship instructed us to compose ourselves and to breathe in and breathe out slowly. Then she began to pray something along these lines:

> Lord, help us to still our hearts and minds, to prepare ourselves to hear whatever you have in store for us. To that end, let us pray to breathe in the Spirit and breathe out pain; breathe in Divine Love and breathe out distress, and fatigue; breathe in Thy mercy and breathe out any evil that may separate us from You; breathe in Thy peace and breathe

out anger; breathe in Thy Light and breathe out all darkness.

In effect we were, individually and corporately, opening ourselves to God and casting away everything that was not of God. This continued for five to ten minutes and resulted in a wonderful sense of peace and contentment that had settled upon the group. We had stilled ourselves through amazing grace to sit at the feet of the cross and listen with our spiritual selves. I thought, "How wonderful!" Then I tried to practice this form of prayer especially when I felt distressed.

My next encounter with meditation came in a Lenten discussion group at Church. This was a group of people who undertook a theological study each week during the period of Lent in special preparation for Easter. One in our group shared her experience of short meditation as part of her prayer life. She asked us to assume very physically relaxed positions, to close our eyes and to concentrate for about five minutes on relaxing the muscles of our bodies, starting from the head down to the toes. We next chose some form of positive input to repetitively "breathe in" and another form of negative output to repetitively "breathe out." For example, breathe in the Peace of the Lord and breathe out anger, hurt, and pain. With eyes still closed, we coordinated our mental breathing in of the good and breathing out of the evil with every physical breath we took for about ten minutes. Then she quietly ended our meditation by asking us to open our eyes, but to remain in our comfortable positions. As we quietly shared our thoughts of the experience, it was apparent that each one of us found value in the stillness and increased sense of peace. Yet, not all of us found that the meditation seemed to bring us closer to God. It was obviously not a useful tool for everyone. However, I was much intrigued.

Later in my life, I entered a period of such emotional distress that I was unable to focus very effectively upon anything. It was during the time of trauma when I first realized that I had been sexually molested as a child. I simply couldn't think or concentrate upon much of anything except the emotional problems at hand. I seemed to just be "spaced out" most of the time, unable to even understand more than a couple minutes of conversation or a few paragraphs of whatever I was reading. I felt quite lost inside.

In order to help me to begin to function more normally, my psychologist encouraged me to practice meditation several times daily so that I might become more able to focus my thoughts. He directed me to read *The Relaxation Response* by Herbert Benson, M.D.[1] to learn about meditation techniques and the physiological and psychological benefits of the practice. I was pleasantly surprised to find my Judeo-Christian roots among the great mystics who practiced meditation in ages past: Ignatius of Antioch, St. Theresa, Rabbi Abulafia, Fray Francisco de Osuna, and Martin Luther, to name a few. The early Russian mystics and later the Greek monks of Mount Athos developed a meditation called the Prayer of the Heart, in which the object of focus is upon the heart while mentally repeating the short prayer, "Lord Jesus Christ, Son of God, have mercy upon me." This is similar to the "Jesus Prayer" of meditation more commonly used today, wherein the person simply prays, "Lord Jesus, have mercy on me", or even more simply uses only the name "Jesus" as a repetitive prayer. I decided that I could learn to meditate, not only as a psychological and physiological benefit, but as a wonderful new method of prayer to enrich my spiritual life.

After a reading Dr. Benson's book and some further thought about the subject, I developed my own style of meditation, which I am more than happy to share with you. It

---

[1] Herbert Benson, M.D., *The Relaxation Response* (New York: Avon Books, a division of The Hearst Corporation, 1976)

includes the primary components of (1) a quiet environment, (2) a comfortable physical position, (3) an object of focus, and (4) a passive attitude.

Environment: It is best to choose a quiet environment and, preferably, to be alone to avoid as much external distraction as possible. Use a quiet place of worship or a private room at home. The object is to seclude yourself, if possible, to avoid people, noise, and activity. Sometimes when I can't retreat from background noise, I use ear plugs.

Physical position: Be comfortable, whatever that means to you. I usually sit in an overstuffed chair with a foot-stool, and an afghan over my legs on a cool day. Some people prefer to sit on the floor with crossed legs. There is no ordained position, but there is one prohibition. Do not lie down to meditate or you may easily fall asleep, thereby ending the meditation prematurely. If you are unable to relax very quickly, then take a few moments to close your eyes, breathe deeply a few times, and command your muscles to relax, starting from the top of your head to the tip of your toes. Be sure you are physically relaxed before attempting to enter the meditation.

Object of focus: Sometimes I gaze upon a crucifix in my hands or a Christian symbol upon the wall. Most often I simply close my eyes and envision the cross. Then I pray repetitively, "Lord, have mercy." I listen to my breathing and time the "Lord" with an intake of breath and the "have mercy" with the exhaled breath. I continue the meditation for ten to twenty minutes, glancing at my watch or a clock occasionally. Then I discontinue the prayer, open my eyes, or look elsewhere from the object upon which I might have been gazing. Meditation commonly slows the body metabolism by reducing oxygen consumption, respiration, heartbeat, and blood pressure among other things. Therefore, it is important to allow the body as well as the mind a few minutes to return to normal. So, don't jump up or move hastily for four or five minutes. Use the time to allow your mind some quiet activity. Sometimes, I read a psalm or a page of inspirational literature. Sometimes I just sit and listen for inspiration, insights and guidance from the Lord.

<u>Passive attitude</u>: It is a natural and common experience to have external thoughts constantly intruding upon the meditation. Please do not let this disturb you and frustrate you. Simply let the thoughts pass through. That is, as soon as you have noticed that your thoughts have wandered from the focus of your meditation, simply and gently return to the focus and not allow yourself to become disturbed. Remain passive to all intrusions. Do not become obsessed with the need to focus, but let the focus and the repetitive prayer flow calmly, serenely from your interior being. Trying too hard can become just another internal obstacle to overcome. Remember that mental stress becomes reflected in the body. Then both body and mind lose the comfortable relaxation necessary to succeed.

"Let go and let God" is an old saying that applies to meditation. Try to let go of yourself so that you may let God into yourself and be able to receive whatever He has in store for you. Because of the abandonment of self that is accomplished during meditation, it becomes possible to hear the Lord more clearly. That is, the communication channels seem sometimes to become a bit unclogged so that a person will often find answers, inspiration, guidance, and spiritual comfort after meditation. This did not happen to me immediately, although I did succeed in relaxing and receiving some of the Lord's peace even upon my first attempt. I tried to meditate at least daily for an entire week before I felt I had any success. I imagine the learning curve differs with each individual, and I encourage you to keep trying for many times. You will know when you have succeeded when you realize that your respiration and oxygen intake is significantly reduced, you feel completely relaxed, and your mind and spirit seem at peace.

The ancient mystics often wrote of reaching a spiritual ecstasy through the abandonment of self. I'm not sure what this ecstasy is supposed to feel like, and I certainly would not presume to label my meditative experiences with the term "ecstasy." Perhaps I have never reached their levels of spiritual insight. It has never been my goal to reach ecstasy. My only purpose has been to focus on prayer, to seek my Lord, and to commune with him.

I remember a vision I received during one of my first attempts at meditation. I had been focusing upon a mental image of the cross and praying, "Jesus, have mercy." I saw a woman kneeling in prayer not far from the foot of the cross. She was wearing an apron, and I identified myself with her because of my own small kitchen ministry. Behind the cross a very bright light appeared, and the source of the light was too bright for me to look at directly. The light beamed through the cross, and as it passed through the cross its intensity diminished so that I could tolerate seeing it. It fell upon the woman (myself) who received it with outstretched arms. Then the scene shifted. I beheld a dark cloud with lightening flashing. It changed into a white cloud raining golden raindrops. Then everything in my field of vision turned into a golden mist.

I found the vision very comforting. The imagery of the woman praying at the foot of the cross reflected my own prayer efforts. The light that was too bright to look at directly was a symbol of my Creator God, who loved me so much that he sent his son to redeem me. Through Jesus, symbolized by the cross, I was able to see God and to receive divine love and mercy. Of course, the dark cloud with lightening symbolized the storm in my life. And as the cloud changed to the color of white with the gold rain, I understood the symbolical moment to be healing, for in my dreams white is the color of healing. The rain of gold shows me the redemption of pain into something of value. Finally, when everything turned golden, I understood that through the Holy Spirit all of my life and all of my sufferings will be sanctified.

Please note that I did not immediately understand this vision which required prayer, contemplation, and plain old wondering to root out the meaning. The things of God are not like modern fast food service. One must spend time with the Lord and time thinking upon the things of God, such as his living word, the Bible.

On Contemplation

In the context of prayer, I would define contemplation as pondering or pensively thinking upon God, his creation, and his living word in relation to myself. It is a thought process through which I attempt to find meaning and spiritual revelation of life. I believe contemplation is prayer, because it is an attempt to gain insight and to communicate with the Lord by learning to understand him through his teachings and through his creation. Contemplation has to do with where and how I find my Lord and how this affects my life.

Not long ago I went on retreat with an ecumenical group to Cape Cod. During one of the breaks between sessions, we strolled upon the sand dunes of North Eastham. It was a lovely interlude and a time to pause and look at God's creation of the sea. I chanced to look down upon a small rock in the sand. It was a common rock upon that windy shore, and it was rounded from the pounding of the sea. As I picked it up, I looked at the rock and thought about biblical symbols.

> The Lord is my rock, my fortress, and my deliverer,
> my God, my rock in whom I take refuge,
> my shield, and the horn of my salvation, my stronghold.
>
> *Psalm 18:2 (NRSV)*

Then for the rest of the day I began to notice rocks in song and scripture. "He alone is my rock and my salvation..." (Psalm 62:2) And, I thought about the nature of rocks and the nature of our creator God.

God provides us with a firm foundation for life. He is a rock made of solid stuff. He is always there to give us the strength and courage we need in times of trouble. He protects and shelters us from the storms of life, and He is our hope when we have no other.

As I pursued my contemplation, I also remembered reading the parable of the vine and the branches.

> Take care to live in me, and let me live in you. For a branch can't produce fruit when severed from the vine. Nor can you be fruitful apart from me.
>
> Yes, I am the Vine; you are the branches. Whoever lives in me and I in him shall produce a large crop of fruit. For apart from me you can't do a thing.
>
> *John 15:4-5 (TLB)*

Two thoughts struck me. First of all, the viability of the vine and the branch as a living entity really depends upon the branch remaining on the vine. The branch dies without the vine. However, the vine does not die when the branch is pruned. It will simply produce another branch to bear fruit. If Jesus is the vine and we are the branches, then our spiritual life force comes from Him, and we are integrated with Him. We have become a part of Him as He has become a part of us. Secondly, this can only happen if we allow it, that is, if we take care to abide in Him and allow Him to abide in us.

Now, what does this vine parable have to do with the rock? Think about it. When you abide in Christ and allow Him to abide in you, you become a part of the rock, for Jesus is the cornerstone and the rock of your spiritual foundation. You are somehow integrated into Christ as Christ becomes integrated into you. Then through the power of the Holy Spirit you have access to all of the amazing grace you need. You become a part of the rock as the rock of salvation has become a part of you. You can be strong in the spirit and strong in the Lord!

I shared these contemplative thoughts with my friend Lori, who had battled with breast cancer. I gave her the rock to keep as a symbol of the strength of Christ, which abides in her through her precious gift of faith. Lori had already been walking hand in hand with the Lord through her personal hell, but I had never before recognized her courage. Then I began to understand her walk in spiritual victory over the radiation treatments and all the other ugly battles of her war. Not only has she inspired me, but Lori has shown me the living truth of the vine and the branch and becoming a part of the rock of salvation.

On the Prayer Journal

Believe it or not, composition has always been one of my lesser skills. The notion of writing this book was not of my own choosing because composition comes slowly to me. I am a much more articulate speaker and have no qualms addressing crowds of people. It is the unfilled page that intimidates me. Therefore, it should come as no surprise that I have very little experience with any type of personal journal.

When I was discussing my book outline with my friend Mary, she cautioned me not to forget the personal journal as a means of prayer. I had to admit she was right. However, that meant I had either to write about something I had not yet personally experienced or I had to learn to compose a journal in order to write about it with some personal knowledge and experience. I had previously tried to maintain a journal of my dreams as a method of psychological therapy and development, but I had failed to accomplish this successfully. Mary persisted. She promised to teach me and to "hold my hand" through my first experiences. She insisted that the prayer journal was an entirely different experience from any other form of journal and that difference might enable me to overcome my difficulties. She was right.

Basically, to write a journal effectively, a person must quickly record the thoughts that well up. Get words on paper. Birth the thoughts. Do not pay any attention to spelling, punctuation, or grammar. That's where my problem lay. Years of secretarial and administrative tasks held me prisoner to editing as I compose. Therefore, my thoughts tend to become convoluted, stymied, and finally pent-up because I cannot explode with them. At least, all of this was true until I learned to offer up the task as a prayer. Then, once again, the Lord was able to change my life. I must admit this is still not my favorite form of prayer, but nevertheless, I have enjoyed it and benefited from the fruits of my labor.

The following technique of journalizing reflects what Mary taught me. First of all, there must be a prayer or at least a sound intention of offering the journal as a prayer unto the Lord. It can even be undertaken as an intercessory effort. For example, Mary offered her journal for years in support of a member of her family. You may simply want to offer the journal as an expression of praise and thanksgiving. Whatever your intention, just remember to approach the task in a reverent attitude of prayer.

<u>Step One:</u> Prayerfully select a portion of scripture to read. If you are doing this daily, you may want to consider using an Old Testament reading one day and alternate it with a New Testament the next day. The length of the reading is up to you. I would suggest that you not read for more than five to ten minutes. The scriptures are not light reading. Read slowly and pensively.

<u>Step Two</u>: Begin to write your thoughts concerning what-

ever you have read. Just let the words flow. Do not try to compose. Just write the words as they flow through your mind. Forget about grammar, punctuation, and syntax. "Go with the flow of the Spirit" as best you can. If you wish, refer back to the Word as often or as little as you like, maybe not at all. If your thoughts wander a bit, you might want to write them, too. Simply write until you feel "done." This is usually accomplished in about twenty minutes.

Step Three: End the exercise by writing a brief prayer. This brings closure to your task by affirming and focusing upon the prayer. Effectively, you have begun the journal as an offering and have ended by a completion of prayer. Amen.

I accepted my friend's invitation to lead me through the writing of my first prayer and to share the experience with me. Now I wish to share my first prayer journal with you. It is fairly short, clear and concise.

Step One: We began with reading Psalm 63, which Mary had already selected.

> O God, you are my God, I seek you, my soul
>   thirsts for you;
> my flesh faints for you, as in a dry and weary
>   land where there is no water.
> So I have looked upon you in the sanctuary,
>   beholding your power and glory.
> Because your steadfast love is better than life
>   my lips will praise you.
> So I will bless you as long as I live;
>   I will lift up my hands and call on your name.
> My soul is satisfied as with a rich feast, and my
>   mouth praises you with joyful lips
> when I think of you on my bed, and meditate on
>   you in the watches of the night;
> for you have been my help, and in the shadow of
>   your wings I sing for joy.

My soul clings to you; your right hand upholds
   me.
But those who seek to destroy my life shall go
   down into the depths of the earth;
they shall be given over to the power of the
   sword, they shall be prey for jackals.
But the king shall rejoice in God; all who swear
   by him shall exult, for the mouths of liars will
   be stopped.
Psalm 63 (NRSV)

<u>Step Two</u>: Next we began to compose our thoughts with as little hesitation as possible. I wrote the following:

David seeks the Lord in a dry and weary land as I seek the Lord during my wilderness experiences of life. I cannot also find the energy to seek Him & He has to find me and lead me. I cannot always see Him or hear Him, but I know He is there. O Lord, comfort me. Love me. Wipe my inward unshed tears. Heal my soul.

I have known your miracles in the past and I have glorified you for them. It gives me hope for the future. Without you there is little hope.

Today I worshipped you alongside others at Sunday service. I felt your presence in the sanctuary. I saw your love in other people. I gave your love to the widow in tears. Thank you for the words to her.

Thank you for the encouragement to write. Not one, but two people were grateful for the newsletter articles. I was thinking about discontinuing them (a little) at least on a regular basis, but I guess you want me to continue. Thanks for the guidance. Praise you Lord. Thank you.

v.7. Because you are my help... I can only write effectively, fruitfully, honorably—because you are my help.

Those who criticize me in my work for you will be labeled fools when full knowledge comes to all of us in time. There will be a day of reckoning in your plan, in your season.

v.11 But the king will rejoice in God, and I will rejoice in God, and all of us who seek the face of the Lord—who truly seek Him—will rejoice in the knowledge of God. Those who are not with us will be silenced.

<u>Step Three</u>: I ended by writing the following small prayer of thanksgiving:

Prayer: Thank you, Lord, for bringing me to Mary's house for this my first experience in journalizing. It was lovely to have her "holding my hand" and guiding me with love.

When I finished I was so excited! I had actually done it! I had completed a journal entry without getting all hung up by the proprieties of writing. It must have been the sacrifice of prayer that helped me to overcome all of my well-established inhibitions. God had broken through. Praise and thank Him! I had broken ground on a new avenue of prayer and could communicate in a new manner.

Why is this mystical? I began by describing the scripture, and then I transitioned to "talking" to God about it through my written words. Lastly, I integrated the scripture into my own life. This was not my plan, but did it just happen? I certainly was not in control. As a matter of fact, I was striving desperately to let go of any controls. If I was not in control, who was? It had to have been the Lord, and therein lay the mystery and the mysticism of my prayer journal.

In Summary, Christian mysticism began with Jesus and was a natural extension of the mysteries of God and the mysticism found in the Old Testament. As believers, we are part of the mystical Body of Christ here on earth. This is not logical; it is spiritual. It is a position of faith and a truth realized through communion with God.

Meditation is not confined to the study of scripture. We can use meditation to practice the presence of the Lord near to us, to seek his face, and to receive his peace. It is a means of putting aside one's self and concentrating on Him. Prayerful meditation often leads to communing with the Lord, perhaps receiving a sudden insight, healing, guidance, or peace.

In my own little world, contemplation means finding God everywhere I choose to look—in His creation, in other people, in the events of my everyday life. It not only means thinking upon the things of God, but thinking about God in all things.

Beginning with a prayer and ending with a prayer, the journal can be an exciting new adventure in communicating with the Lord. The key is letting go and letting God take control of the pen.

Questions for Discussion:

1. A dramatic example of Christian mysticism is the Transfiguration as recorded in the gospels of Matthew 17:1-21, Mark 9:2-29, and Luke 9:28-43. Read as least one of these versions and discuss how you may have felt if you were there.

2. Have you ever had an experience in which you recognized the presence of God, but you really did not understand what he was doing? Discuss your experience.

3. Real Psalms 48:9, 119:15, and 143:5. Using the technique described in this chapter, attempt a group meditation facilitated by the group leader or someone who has a little experience in meditation. Discuss the results among yourselves.

4. Think upon the things of God and ask him to show you his hand upon your life. You may very well be surprised with the intimacy of contemplation.

5. I encourage each reader to attempt a prayer journal each day for a week. Use the guidelines established in Chapter Six or go to a Christian bookstore to find a more comprehensive study on the subject. A group effort is beneficial for the first attempt at using the journal as a method of prayer.

CHAPTER EIGHT

The Laying On of Hands

Lord, please give me the words to lead others into thoughts and prayers to use with the laying on of hands. Let no one be confused or intimidated by the gift of touch. But let all flow smoothly and simply from the Holy Spirit through the heart in love.

On the Simple Explanation

I initially thought the laying on of hands sounded like an ominous event. It is not. It is simply another form of praying for one another. The person receiving the prayer is physically touched by those who are praying for him. The laying on of hands can be as casual as simply joining hands to pray, or as formal as the liturgical sacramental rite of Confirmation, wherein the bishop lays both hands upon the head of the confirmand. In any event, it is not something to fear. It is simply a loving touch of prayer.

However, before we explore the subject further, I'd like to make a little side trip into the use of hands in communication and the importance of using hands between people.

On the Remarkable Hand

Our hands usually are very expressive of ourselves. They lend body language to all we say and do. Think of the clenched fist in anger, the outreached hands of a beggar, the open hands of a child gleefully receiving a cookie, the wave of fond greeting or sad farewell, and the hands held reverently in a posture of prayer. How many people do you know that use their hands to "talk" as they speak in conversation. I talk with my hands almost all the time. It is ingrained in me and is a part of my personality. I also like to reach out and touch my friends occasionally. It's part of my linkage with them and my self-extension to those for whom I care very much.

It is this touching of another that proves so powerful between persons. We give and receive physical sensations as well as emotional communications through our hands. The mother's hands gently stroking a distressed child is as important as anything she is verbally telling that child. The loving touch of her hand quells the fears and quiets the child. Think of lovers and how they communicate their love through touching one another. I am not sure that any of us is capable of loving someone without touching in one way or another. We human beings are simply made to somehow touch one another as we connect our lives together in any form of intimacy. It seems natural to us unless we have been damaged or abused by the touch of another. The physical touch of one to another can become a powerful channel of communication ranging from abuse to love to healing.

On the Touch of Jesus

Jesus often touched those he healed. Let us review some of those healings:

> ...and there was a leper who came to him and knelt before him, saying, "Lord, if you choose, you can make me clean." He stretched out his hand and *touched* him, saying, "I do choose. Be made clean!"

The Laying On of Hands

> Immediately his leprosy was cleansed.
> *Matt. 8:2-3 (NRSV)*

> When Jesus entered Peter's house, he saw his mother-in-law lying in bed with a fever; he *touched* her hand, and the fever left her, and she got up and began to serve him.
> *Matt. 8:14-15 (NRSV)*

> They brought to him a deaf man who had an impediment in his speech; and they begged him to lay his hand on him. He took him aside in private, away from the crowd, and put his fingers into his ears, and he spat and *touched* his tongue. Then looking up to heaven, he sighed and said to him "Ephphatha," that is, "Be opened." And immediately his ears were opened, his tongue was released, and he spoke plainly.
> *Mark 7:32-35 (NRSV)*

Whomever Jesus touched was healed, and whoever touched him was healed. It appeared that the healing power of God was often conveyed through a simple touch.

Consider the woman with the hemorrhage:

> Now there was a woman who had been suffering from hemorrhages for twelve years; and though she had spent all she had on physicians, no one could cure her. She came up behind him and touched the fringe of his clothes, and immediately her hemorrhage stopped. Then Jesus asked, "Who touched me?" When all denied it, Peter said, "Master, the crowds surround you and press in on you." But Jesus said, "Someone touched me; for I noticed that power had gone out from me." When

the woman saw that she could not remain hidden, she came trembling; and falling down before him, she declared in the presence of all the people why she had touched him, and how she had been immediately healed. He said to her, "Daughter, your faith has made you well; go in peace."
Luke 8:43-48 (NRSV)

Jesus immediately felt the connection, even through the fringe of his clothes. He had been touched and, therefore, linked to another person for just a moment. That touch was a prayer beyond the power of words. It was an act of faith through which God bestowed healing power.

In biblical times, the laying on hands was always a gesture symbolic of the giving and receiving of a spiritual gift. When Jesus blessed the little children, "he took them up in his arms, laid his hands on them, and blessed them." (Mark 10:16, NRSV) In the Book of Acts, the apostles sent Peter and John to Samaria to pray for those who had accepted the word of God. "Then Peter and John laid their hands on them, and they received the Holy Spirit." (Acts 8:17, NRSV) Later the Apostle Paul instructs Timothy, "Do not neglect the gift that is in you, which was given to you through prophecy with the laying on of hands by the council of elders." (I Tim:14, NRSV) Regarding the ordination of leaders, Paul further cautioned him, "Be in no hurry to lay hands on someone to dedicate him to the Lord's service." (I Tim. 5:22, Good News Bible)

On the Practice Used Today

Just as many of our sacramental and liturgical rituals have been passed down from the apostles to us today, so it is with the laying on of hands. It is commonly used in the sacraments such as confirmation, in which the bishop lays hands upon the candidate to accept his adult commitment to Christ and to the community of the Church and to pray for the spiritual blessing of the Holy Spirit in that person's life. Again, in the sacrament of ordination, the bishop lays hands upon the candidate's head to pray, to bless and to consecrate that person to the priesthood. In many of the churches, it is common to witness the pastor or priest laying one or both hands upon the head of a person in a simple blessing. It is also common in services of consecration or dedication of a person's work in the service of Our Lord.

Perhaps the most common usage of the laying on of hands today is in the healing ministry, where the focus of prayer is on spiritual, mental or physically healing. Following the example of Jesus Christ, many Christians will lay hands upon those whom they are lifting up in prayer for healing. There is nothing "spooky" about it, and there should never be anything theatrical in the laying on of hands. However, this tradition has been highly abused, warped, and misused in various areas of Christendom today to the extent that many Christians sincerely believe that it is not a Godly practice. These people will admit that Jesus and the apostles did lay hands upon the sick to heal them, but they will also claim that such a practice was only useful and appropriate during apostolic times. If the reader is of that opinion, then he or she may become uncomfortable reading the rest of this chapter. Nevertheless, I believe that any discourse on prayer would be incomplete without including the laying on of hands for the purpose of healing.

My thoughts return to memories of my children when they were sick. I would often hold them and rock them. How natural it was to stroke them lovingly with my hands and to pray for them to become well. I'm sure that my presence and my love brought comfort to the sick child, but it was the healing touch of Our Lord that restored their health. My daughter Laura was the first to understand this. Sometimes when she felt miserably ill with flu or asthma, she would ask me to sit on the side of her bed and pray for her. Then I would lay my hand on her forehead and speak aloud, asking Jesus to come into the room, to touch Laura, and to make her feel better. Usually she felt comforted and fell asleep right after the prayer.

My family tradition and my Christian tradition for many years was to seek medication and the doctor. When all else failed, start to pray. Happily, I have learned better. I now pray first; then I seek pharmaceutical or medical assistance. Mine is not a position of either faith healing or medical healing, but of both because both have come from Our Lord.

> Honor physicians for their services, for the Lord created them;
> for their gift of healing comes from the Most High, and they are rewarded by the king.
> The skill of physicians makes them distinguished, and in the presence of the great they are admired.
> The Lord created medicines out of the earth, and the sensible will not despise them.
> Was not water made sweet with a tree in order that its power might be known?
> And he gave skill to human beings that he might be glorified in his marvelous works.
> By them the physician heals and takes away pain; the pharmacist makes a mixture from them.
> God's works will never be finished; and from him health spreads over all the earth.
> My child, when you are ill, do not delay, but pray to the Lord, and he will heal you.
> Give up your faults and direct your hands rightly, and cleanse your heart from all sin.
> Offer a sweet-smelling sacrifice, and a memorial portion of choice flour, and pour oil on your

offering, as much as you can afford.
Then give the physician his place, for the Lord
created him; do not let him leave you, for you
need him.
There may come a time when recovery lies in the
hands of physicians, for they too pray to the
Lord that he grant them success in diagnosis
and in healing, for the sake of preserving life.
He who sins against his Maker, will be defiant
toward the physician.
Apocryphal Book of Sirach 38:1-15 (NRSV)

In the light of God's gift of medicine, I become frustrated with those Christians who deny medicine and teach that healing is contingent upon a person's faith. Our Lord is perfectly capable of healing those of little or no faith as well as those of great faith. He can heal with the doctor and without the doctor. Nevertheless, I do believe that Jesus respects the individual and grants any person the right to refuse healing. However, it is his business who to heal, where to heal, how to heal and when to heal. We cannot exercise guidelines and restrictions upon God.

In the beginning of that season when I learned to pray for healing, I developed very red and sore gums throughout my mouth. I mentioned this condition to a well-meaning and goodhearted Christian friend who advised me that I did not need to see a doctor or a dentist. I just needed prayer to heal my mouth. So, he laid hands on me prayed for my healing; and I prayed for myself for several days. As the condition began to improve, I thought my friend was right! I had visions of saving all kinds of money, time, and energy by avoiding medicine and just using my newfound faith to heal my body. My daydreams dissipated shortly, when I discovered a very loose tooth and rushed to the dentist. I had developed severe periodontal problems throughout my mouth and consequently lost a perfectly healthy molar due to gum disease. If I had sought medical attention when I noticed my red gums, the tooth could probably have been saved. Now I have a permanent dental bridge to remind me of that lesson. The Lord will not have me trying to control how he wants to heal me.

Most of the time I have experienced the laying on of hands has been in small prayer groups usually connected to Bible study or devotional programs. A few years ago, five of us women began to meet weekly in an ongoing support group for recovery from abuse. We were all mature women and mature Christians who had known and loved the Lord for a very long time. We were all survivors of much abuse in the past—physical, mental, verbal, sexual, or a combination of these things. Most of us had shared these griefs with our pastors and priests and had received their understanding and prayer support. In addition to spiritual guidance, we all had mental health counseling, therapy, and/or medication. It had always been our purpose to combine healing prayer with medical help. We were not strangers when we began to meet, so there was one less obstacle to forming a cohesive support group, and it seemed a little easier to pray for each other as we knew something about one another, even from the beginning.

We began each meeting with general prayers of praise and thanksgiving, and we lifted ourselves up to the Lord, asking him to help us to receive whatever he wanted to show us. We prayed that he would guide our thoughts and our prayers to insights and healing from on high. And, we asked God to pour the Holy Spirit upon us to do the work he had prepared for us to accomplish. Sometimes we sang a gospel tune or two, sometimes not. However, we prayed for at least ten to twenty minutes, usually until we realized the peace of the Lord upon us. Then we read a devotional passage of scripture with a recovery theme. We discussed our personal responses or reactions to that reading, sometimes discover-

The Laying On of Hands

ing new insights into our pain or healing. Next we read aloud the commentary and teaching prepared by a theologian and psychologist regarding this scripture; and we discussed how this might apply to our lives. We concluded our session with the laying on of hands.

We placed a chair in the center of the room and took turns occupying it. Whoever occupied the chair was the subject and focus of our group prayer. One person stood behind the chair and laid both hands upon the subject's head, and the rest of us simply gathered round, also touching the subject. Sometimes that person requested specific prayers, sometimes not. The person standing behind the chair began to pray out loud as she led the rest of us into prayer. Each of us took a turn praying out loud. We all felt free to pray in support of that person's need and in accordance to the Holy Spirit. Whoever was sitting in the chair did not usually pray for herself, but simply opened herself to receive the spiritual movement of our prayers and the blessing of the Lord upon her. It was a precious moment, an intimate moment with God and with each other. And we were grateful to be so blessed from on high.

Something spiritual always happens, even if we don't immediately understand it. We receive healing in some dimension, whether it is physical, mental or spiritual, whether we receive it during the laying on of hands or subsequent to that moment. It is all connected to Love's presence among us as Our Lord Jesus is there touching us and healing us. If we are willing, he directs and guides us through our prayers and the laying on of hands. It is a sacred event, not to be approached lightly. Remember that Jesus loves us and empowers us to love one another with the love of God.

An even more casual approach to this laying on of hands can be accomplished by simply forming a circle and holding hands with each other in prayer. It is the touching and the central focus of the group upon the same person as the subject of prayer that is important. The touching is an act of love through which spiritual power flows from the source of all true love. And we don't even have to "feel" anything for it to happen. We just have to be available to the Lord and to reach out to one another. This can be just as powerful with only two people holding hands in prayer as it is with a group. It's really up to the Lord to decide when and where to heal, guide, and instruct us. However, it has been my observation that the most powerful events seem to occur where there is corporate prayer and praise, that is, where many people are gathered together in his name.

I have witnessed the laying on of hands with dramatic healing in Eucharistic healing services with liturgy, at revival tent meetings, in Full Gospel meetings, in both ecumenical and denominational settings, and in conservative as well as charismatic events. The Lord's hand moves as he wills, whether we approve of the company or not.

Remember that Jesus was considered a radical and a troublemaker when he walked this earth. He even talked to Gentiles and ate with sinners and tax collectors. How can we expect him to respect our guidelines for "appropriate behavior" today? His love has no boundaries! Praise the Lord!

My friend Arlene is a wonderful example of healing with the laying on of hands. She and her husband Les were attending a Full Gospel Businessmen's dinner meeting about ten years ago. After the dinner and the speaker, there was a period of prayer and the laying on of hands to all who requested. The prayer teams were at the front of the room where there was much spiritual activity, but Arlene was standing at the back of the room when another lady approached her and began to talk to her. She noticed that Arlene had a cast in her left eye and asked her about it. Arlene admitted that she had suffered this weakness all of her life and that she had been wearing eyeglasses since the first grade due to astigmatism and nearsightedness. The lady announced that she believed that the Lord would want Arlene's eyes healed, and she asked Arlene for permission to pray and lay hands upon her. Arlene agreed and removed her eyeglasses. The lady laid her hands over Arlene's eyes and prayed very simply for the Lord to heal her eyes. Arlene also prayed inwardly that it be the Lord's will to heal her and that she would have the faith to receive the healing. She felt waves of spiritual peace moving over her body from head to foot, and she knew that she had been touched by God. When I approached her a few minutes later, I noticed she had been crying. But she explained that she was crying from joy because the Lord had healed her eyes. I said, "Really, that's wonderful!" But, I was just being polite. I didn't see anything different about Arlene's cast eye, and I was skeptical that she was emotionally high from prayer. Little did I know!

When she began to drive home, Arlene noticed that she could not see the road very well, nor could she read the signs easily. She knew that she was driving erratically, but didn't understand what was wrong until she realized that she could no longer see properly with her glasses. As soon as she removed her eyeglasses, she could see perfectly well to resume her driving safely. It was a miracle! For the first time in forty years, Arlene did not need glasses. She even had to go back to the registry to have her eyes tested to remove the driving restriction of eyeglasses from her driver's license.

Two days after the meeting, I visited Arlene at her office and noticed that her left eye had begun to move toward the proper alignment in the center. Within two to three weeks, that eye corrected itself without medical attention. To this day, Arlene's eyes are perfectly aligned with just a hint of a cast only when she is extremely tired. It is that occasional hint of a cast that reminds me of God's power to heal and the living proof of that healing in my friend.

Break Ground

In Summary, giving the touch of a hand or receiving someone's touch is a remarkable experience of many layers. It is more than a simple sensory input or expression of body language. The touch of a hand can also be an extension of oneself to another in body, soul, and spirit.

Not only did Jesus use the laying on of hands during his ministry, but he taught the apostles to do the same, and even commanded the laying on of hands through visions after his ascension into heaven. He reached out to touch most of those he healed, even though he could have healed them from afar. This was not necessary, but it was the method he chose and modeled for his followers and for us today.

Therefore, I encourage you to listen to the Lord and to touch, hold hands or lay hands upon those in need of healing, whenever the opportunity permits. If it is His will, the Lord will make a way for you. Just be obedient.

Questions for Discussion:

1. Take a moment to discuss how you personally use your hands in communication with other people. How do you use your hands when communicating with the Lord?

2. When do you find yourself using your hands deliberately to touch others? (Example: the handshake binding an agreement)

3. Jesus used his hands to bless and to create all sorts of miracles, especially healing. Read Mark 5:35-43. Note how Jesus touched the girl.

4. Read the story of Ananias in Acts 9:10-19. The Lord gave visions to both Paul and Ananias ordaining that Ananias was to "lay hands" upon Paul to both restore his physical sight and to baptize him with the Holy Spirit.

The Laying On of Hands

5. Now read Acts 13:1-3 for a Biblical example of commissioning a ministry. Note that the leaders fasted, prayed, and then laid hands upon Paul and Barnabus. How do you and the people of your church use the "laying on of hands" today?

6. If the group feels comfortable, hold hands and pray for healing for each other.

CHAPTER NINE

Praying in Tongues

Lord, it hurts to see your gift of tongues so sadly misunderstood and abused. It is no wonder that so many Christians want nothing to do with tongues or those who practice this form of prayer. Grant me the insight and the courage to teach them differently. Thank you.

On the Definition of Glossolalia

The gift of tongues is also known as glossolalia (glah-so-la-lee-lah). It is the ability to speak a language that the speaker does not himself understand. If you don't know anything about it, tongues is just a bunch of nonsensical babbling. As understood through the eyes of faith, glossolalia is a prayer language received from the Holy Spirit to be used for the glory of God and the building of his kingdom here on earth. Yet this gift from God has been much neglected by the majority of Christendom in modern times. Even when it is used, it is often used improperly, resulting in controversy and alienation among the people of God. Unfortunately, tongues have been misused to cause pain and hurt, instead of love and healing. How has this happened? How did this come to be?

On the Biblical Roots

Probably the best place to begin to unravel misconceptions is a look at the biblical roots of glossolalia, starting with the Old Testament and the story of the Tower of Babel:

> Now the whole earth had one language and the same words. And as they migrated from the east, they came upon a plain in the land of Shinar and settled there. And they said to one another, "Come, let us make bricks, and burn them thoroughly." And they had brick for stone, and bitumen for mortar. Then they said, "Come, let us build ourselves a city, and a tower with its top in the heavens, and let us make a name for ourselves; otherwise we shall be scattered abroad upon the face of the whole earth." The Lord came down to see the city and the tower, which mortals had built. And the Lord said, "Look, they are one people, and they have all one language; and this is only the beginning of what they will do; nothing that they propose to do will now be impossible for them. Come, let us go down, and confuse their language there, so that they will not understand one another's speech." So the Lord scattered them abroad from there over the face of all the earth, and they left off building the city. Therefore it was called Babel, because there the Lord confused the language of all the earth; and from there the Lord scattered them abroad over the face of all the earth.
>
> *Gen. 11:1-9 (NRSV)*

Whether or not this is a mythological account of the origin of languages, it is significant to note that it is the first recorded biblical event in which the Lord takes control of the tongues and utterances of the people. It seems logical that this story with its setting at the Tower of Babel somehow connects to the root of the word babble, which means fabricated and nonsensical speech. After all, no one could understand the other's speech or recognize it as a structured language.

In the New Testament, we find the gift of tongues described in the longer version of the Gospel of Mark as a sign of holiness. The time was after the resurrection of Christ and before his ascension into heaven. Jesus appeared to the remaining eleven apostles and "upbraided them for their lack of faith and stubbornness," (Mark 16:14, NRSV). He exhorted them to go forth to preach the good news, and he further encouraged them with the following words:

> And these signs will accompany those who believe: by using my name they will cast out demons; they will speak in new tongues; they will pick up snakes in their hands, and if they drink any deadly thing, it will not hurt them; they will lay their hands on the sick, and they will recover.
> *Mark 16:17-18 (NRSV)*

The proclamation that they will speak in new tongues was at this point a prophecy. Then Jesus ascended into heaven.

> And they went out and proclaimed the good news everywhere, while the Lord worked with them and confirmed the message by the signs that accompanied it.
> *Mark 16: 20 (NRSV)*

These signs might have included the new tongues. But exactly when did they start? Did the disciples go forth immediately that very day? Perhaps they waited a short period of time, simply praying together or preparing to journey forth. Exactly when did they start speaking in their new languages as a confirming sign of their power in Christ?

The Bible teaches us that the gift of tongues was received by the disciples on the day of Pentecost, seven weeks after Passover and after the ascension of Our Lord.

> When the day of Pentecost had come, they were all together in one place. And suddenly from heaven there came a sound like the rush of a violent wind, and it filled the entire house where they were sitting. Divided tongues, as of fire, appeared among them, and a tongue rested on each of them. All of them were filled with the Holy Spirit and began to speak in other languages, as the Spirit gave them ability.
> *Acts 2:1-4 (NRSV)*

The wind and the divided tongues were physical signs of the presence of the Holy Spirit coming upon them and resting upon each individual. Note that all of the disciples and their followers were filled with the Holy Spirit first. This came in fulfillment of the prophecy of John the Baptist.

> ...I baptize you with water; but one who is more powerful than I is coming; I am not worthy to untie the thong of his sandals. He will baptize you with the Holy Spirit and fire."
> *Luke 3:16 (NRSV)*

It was immediately <u>after</u> their Baptism of the Holy Spirit that the followers of Christ began to speak in new tongues. The gift of tongues proved to be an affirmation from God that the Holy Spirit had truly come to abide in them.

The people outside heard the sounds, and a crowd quickly gathered. They were amazed to hear the Galilean disciples speaking in their own languages and telling them about God's deeds of power. At this point, the gift of tongues was manifested as a structured language understood by those who were listening. The scripture does not clearly indicate that the speakers themselves understood the languages issuing from their own mouths. It might have been. It might not have been. We do know that the experience of Pentecost was an empowering experience, if only through observing Peter. The big fisherman arose with spiritual authority to proclaim the fulfillment of the prophecy of Joel. He further astounded the crowd by proclaiming the good news of Jesus Christ, of his resurrection from the dead, and of his ascension into heaven to sit at the right hand of God. "Therefore let the entire house of Israel know with certainty that God has made him both Lord and Messiah, this Jesus whom you crucified," (Acts 2:36, NRSV).

It is also noteworthy that Peter at this point combines baptism in the name of Jesus Christ with receiving the gift of the Holy Spirit. Apparently the baptism of the new followers of Christ was no longer to be just a baptism of water, but also a baptism of the Holy Spirit affirmed by the gift of tongues. This even caused some backtracking to Samaria where the people had accepted the word of God and had been baptized in the name of Jesus, but had not yet received the Holy Spirit. "Then Peter and John laid their hands on them, and they received the Holy Spirit. " (Acts 8:17, NRSV) How was it immediately evidenced, if not by the gift of tongues?

This is no longer practiced in the mainstream churches of Christianity today. All of them still practice baptism by water, but not all of them recognize the baptism of the Holy Spirit. The liturgical churches have separated these events into the two sacraments of Baptism and Confirmation, with the sacrament of Confirmation being the event by which an adult commits himself to Christ and receives the infilling of the Holy Spirit. This sacrament does not contain prayer for the gift of tongues, nor do most of the candidates expect to receive the gift. The liturgical churches as a whole teach the gift of tongues as a tradition mostly used during biblical times, not as a doctrine. Most of the non-liturgical churches also do not recognize the use, nor the appropriateness, of the gift of tongues today. The notable exception is of course the Pentecostal Church, the Assemblies of God, and many of the small New Testament churches that are continually springing up.

Nevertheless, there is a growing movement worldwide throughout Christianity today towards renewal through the Baptism of the Holy Spirit along with receiving the gift of tongues. It is an ecumenical movement began by the Holy Spirit and led by the Holy Spirit. This is not popular among established churches. It makes waves. It bestirs fervor and fury among steadfast conservative minds, who cannot accept this unusual method of prayer. Many even believe that tongues are a gift of the devil, not of God, and there is probably nothing I can say or do to change their minds. The problem is an old one, two thousand years old. To complicate things, many people have abused their gift and flagrantly misused it, causing the alienation of other Christians. Saint Paul contended with the Corinthians on the same issue. More about this later in the chapter.

On the Gifts of the Holy Spirit

In Chapter 12 of his first letter to the Corinthians, Paul teaches that the various manifestations of the Holy Spirit are apportioned among the believers for the common good, and he proceeds to list the gifts of the Spirit as wisdom, knowledge, healing, miracles, prophecy, discernment, tongues, and the interpretation of tongues. He further proclaims, "If I speak in the tongues of mortals and of angels, but do not have love, I am a noisy gong or a clanging cymbal," (I Cor. 13:1, NRSV). It is clearly understood that the gifts of the Holy

Spirit are to be used in love for the glory of God and for building up his church here on earth. In this respect, the gift of tongues is used in two ways: (1) for the edification of the church, especially through the interpretation of tongues, usually in the manner of prophesy during corporate worship, and (2) for private prayer, a communication of the individual's spirit directly onto the Lord.

Since the intent of this book is to enhance the individual's prayer life by exploring the various methods of prayer, it is important that I address the gift of tongues as a tool of prayer. I do not intend to promote an in-depth study on the gifts of the Holy Spirit. However, I cannot ignore them. I must touch briefly upon them, or I will miss one of the most important methods of prayer. He who speaks in tongues is speaking in a language unknown to himself and usually unknown to those who may hear him. Sometimes, this is not so. Upon rare occasions, a listener may actually understand with his mind (interpret without spiritual aid) what is being said. These would be unusual circumstances, perhaps to help the unbeliever. The language (tongue) is always unknown to the speaker. It comes from the Holy Spirit and flows forth from the subconscious, completely bypassing the intellect. Additionally, one who interprets the tongues also receives that interpretation from the Spirit flowing from the subconscious. The interpreter simply releases the message into words understood by himself and usually those present. Seldom can the interpreter repeat the tongues as spoken because he has been solely concentrating upon "hearing" the words in his mind and speaking them quickly . Hearing inwardly and speaking outwardly almost simultaneously allow neither the time or the mental capacity to creatively listen for understanding. At least, this has been my experience.

On Receiving Tongues Today

To my knowledge the gift of tongues today is still received

through the baptism of the Holy Spirit. There is no uniformly prescribed ritual and few things seem to be required. First of all, the supplicant, or person who seeks the baptism, must have made a commitment to follow Jesus Christ as Lord and Savior of his life. Then it is simply a question of asking, that is, prayer for Our Lord to baptize with his Holy Spirit. Usually one or more persons who have already received the baptism in the Spirit will lay hands upon the supplicant and pray for the baptism. Sometimes this will include prayer for the gift of tongues, sometimes not. Sometimes prayer language comes immediately, whether or not requested in the prayers. Sometimes the person does not want the gift, and Our Lord does not force it upon him. And sometimes, the newly baptized receives the gift without manifestation of it. That is, the gift abides within him, but he has not yet experienced the spiritual release of his prayer language. Only God's timing is perfect for this event.

My own story reflects a lack of structure. Perhaps it is a look at the flexibility of the Holy Spirit, who meets us in all our circumstances of life.

If I believe the liturgy, then I believe that I received the infilling of the Holy Spirit when I was thirteen years old at the sacrament of Confirmation. I knew nothing of tongues outside of the story of Pentecost and did not consider them relevant to modern times. Naturally, I did not receive the gift of tongues at that time.

Twenty-five years later, I found myself in an emotional crisis causing me to feel high levels of anxiety and distress. At a church function, I overheard a couple of people talking excitedly in hushed tones about prayers being answered. I approached them and asked them questions. Feeling a ray of hope, I decided that prayer just might help me. So I asked them to pray for me. They were nervous. However, in complete obedience to the movement of the Holy Spirit, a group of three gathered with me at a table. As we held hands, they

Praying in Tongues

began to pray in a quiet and comforting manner. God touched me, and I cried in relief—not understanding—just knowing a moment of divine love and the love of the prayer team surrounding me. Then they invited me to join their weekly prayer meetings.

It was at those prayer meetings that I began to learn about the gifts of the Holy Spirit in action today. There I learned about laying on hands and praying for healing. There I learned about the baptism of the Holy Spirit as the gateway to empowered prayer through the gift of tongues. These people were new in their gifts, and only Hazel had received the gift of tongues at that time. She was very private with her gift, especially since there was no one there with the gift of interpretation. However, I saw her as living proof that these gifts existed today.

During one of those meetings, I requested specific prayer for a family problem and received the laying on of hands. After hearing the requested prayer, I remember hearing Hazel take a deep breath and nervously pray, "Lord, please baptize Margaret in the Holy Spirit *in your time*." This upset me because I did not feel ready for "a baptism in the Spirit." Yet, I could not object too strenuously, because she had prayed obediently and specifically for the Lord's perfect timing.

A few weeks later I attended an Order of St. Luke meeting with Hazel and the rest of our little group. Our speaker must have been inspired by the Holy Spirit, because she touched me deeply, reminding me of God's love for me and his faithfulness to take care of me. As a deluge of tears arose out of my spiritual brokenness, I felt waves of warmth cascading from my head to my toes. Later I shared the experience with Hazel and asked her if I had been baptized in the Spirit. She said, "I don't really know. I think so. But, why don't you ask God?" I did ask the Lord, but I was not yet able to hear his answer.

Two days later, I was still asking the question and pondering upon events while I washed dishes in my kitchen. I began to reason that I must have received the baptism. The sacrament of Confirmation may have been my original and first infilling of Spirit. However, I knew something had happened to me at that meeting, whether or not it was the baptism or a renewal of spiritual infilling. Perhaps being filled with the Spirit was not a once in the lifetime event. I knew that I had once again committed myself to the Lord and had recently become a new person in Christ Jesus. Therefore, I had been born into new life, and it was my spiritual birthday. So I wanted my birthday present, childlike, pure, and simple. I mentally talked to the Lord, saying, "It's my present, and I want it now. Please, Lord, now. You promised this in your holy word. So, do something." Then I went downstairs to put clothes into the washing machine. In the privacy of my laundry prayer chamber, I tried to pull words out of myself. I started by repeating "Abba, Abba, Abba." Then I would listen for an inward sound or syllable, and try to speak it. It was frustration, incorporated. I ran back upstairs to my kitchen duties, continuing to pray mentally for a release of the Spirit in the gift of tongues. Then later back downstairs for a few minutes of praying out loud. I didn't want the children to hear me, so it was almost like a game of hiding. About the third or fourth trip to the laundry, my tongue sort of tripped over a new sound, and my prayer language was born! Syllables and words came gushing out of me. I cried again—this time in praise and thanksgiving as I fell to my knees.

    I would like to say that a beautiful prayer language, pleasing to the ear, had issued from my mouth. This was not so. What I heard sounded more like a motor coughing and backfiring with a few little honking sounds in between. It was awful to hear, but music to my ears. Perhaps I still had inner barriers to overcome, or perhaps I just had to practice using my new gift. But practice, I did. After a few weeks of praying in tongues at least once a day, I found that my new prayer language began to sound like a structured language, even though I still could not understand it.

On the Use of Tongues Today

As I became comfortable using the gift of tongues, I no longer even thought about the language as I prayed, but simply kept my understanding on thoughts of God while my spirit communed with Him. I discovered the most important thing for me in using this gift. It gives me a means to pray, when I just don't know how to pray in my own words. It is also the resource—available to me at all times—to be able to pray according to the will of God, and not according to the will of Margaret.

When I use the gift of tongues to pray, it is usually a private affair between the Lord and me. Much of the time it is sub vocal, especially if others are present. I usually pray in tongues loudly and with abandon only when I am alone with the Lord. Sometimes I even sing in the prayer language with the Spirit giving me the melody as well as the words. I trust they are pleasing unto God. Once in a great while, I am able to gather with a crowd of other Christians who are comfortable with these gifts. When we begin to pray, sometimes the Holy Spirit will sweep across us in waves and move us to sing in tongues as a sweet chorus of praise and thanksgiving. I always find these occasions a wondrous and awesome event, sharing precious moments of spiritual union with each other and with the Lord.

Unfortunately, not all people use their gift of tongues in spiritual unity, often causing discord and distress among other Christians. It is an old problem dating back to biblical times.

On the Teachings of Paul

Please take the time right now to read First Corinthians, Chapter 14 for an overview of Paul's teachings on the subject of tongues and interpretation of tongues. He appears to be lovingly correcting the Corinthians, who were not using their gifts appropriately and with full responsibility. He begins by encouraging them to seek spiritual gifts.

> For those who speak in a tongue do not speak to other people but to God; for nobody understands them, since they are speaking mysteries in the Spirit. On the other hand, those who prophesy speak to other people for their upbuilding and encouragement and consolation. Those who speak in a tongue build up themselves, but those who prophesy build up the church. Now I would like all of you to speak in tongues, but even more to prophesy. One who prophesies is greater than one who speaks in tongues, unless someone interprets, so that the church may be built up.
>
> *I Cor. 14:2-5 (NRSV)*

Notice that he prioritizes the gift of prophecy over the gift of tongues, although he encourages <u>everyone</u> to speak in tongues. Here he is also referring to the two basic uses of tongues, personal prayer and public prophecy, which can only occur when someone interprets the message that has been delivered in tongues. Remember that the interpretation of tongues is another spiritual gift of the Holy Spirit encouraged by Paul. "Therefore, one who speaks in a tongue should pray for the power to interpret." (v.13)

Problems occur when a person uses the gift of tongues inappropriately, such as interrupting a gathering of worshippers with loud "prophecy in tongues" that no one else can interpret. The Holy Spirit does not send messages without sending the interpretation, and He always does these things in peaceful order. Our spiritual gifts are to be used responsibly. "Let all things be done for building up." (v. 26) There is another unfortunate aspect of these things—the Christian who "shows off" his gifts as a public display of rhapsody with God. I personally receive such behavior (even in church) as vulgar noise. Such behavior is likened unto the Pharisees who prayed on the streets so that everyone could understand how holy and righteous they were supposed to be.

Perhaps the greatest sin of abusing tongues lies within the individual who uses the gift simply to achieve an ecstasy. Of course spiritual ecstasy sometimes occurs, but that too is a gift within the spiritual movement of the Holy Spirit upon the person's soul. It is not an emotional target for an experience of heaven on earth. Some people seek refuge in tongues in almost the same way others seek their highs in drugs or alcohol. They need a reality check. The gift of tongues provides a method of prayer and communication with the Lord for the building of his kingdom on earth. As a spiritual gift, tongues should be used reverently and responsibly, not as a toy or an emotional escape pod.

In Summary, the Lord bestowed the gift of tongues upon his disciples gathered in the upper room on the day of Pentecost. Biblical examples of tongues as a means of prayer abound in the New Testament, where it is found often to be a sign of the believer. Tongues and the interpretation of tongues are gifts of the Holy Spirit; and the Apostle Paul encouraged his followers to use them as an avenue of prayer. However, then as now, the use of these gifts were abused and caused dissention in the Church. Many people began to display their tongues just as the Pharisees displayed their prayers in public for all to see.

Down through the ages the use of tongues has been almost abandoned, to the extent of being uncommon among the mainstream churches. The majority of Christians are uncomfortable with it, and many churches teach that tongues were strictly a biblical phenomena not needed today. However, modern spiritual revival has included the baptism of the Holy

Spirit with the resultant speaking in tongues, breaking new ground for prayer.

Questions for Discussion:

1. Read 1 Cor. 12:1-11. Verse 8 explains the gifts of the Holy Spirit are given for the common good (not only the individual). Note in verse 10 the gifts of tongues and the interpretation of tongues.

2. Have you ever been exposed to someone using the gift of tongues? Did you hear an interpretation? How did you feel about the experience?

3. What does your church teach and practice regarding tongues?

4. Read Acts 19:1-7. What does this scripture teach you about the baptism of the Holy Spirit?

5. If you want to obtain the gift of tongues, first be sure you have already made a commitment to Jesus as Lord of your life. Then have experienced Christians lay hands upon you for the infilling of the Holy Spirit with prayer that you receive the gift of tongues as an affirming gift of divine love.

6. If you have already received this gift, you may want to share some of your experiences with the group.

CHAPTER TEN

According to the Holy Spirit

Lord, direct me along the right path. I can only pray with you as my guide. I can only write with you as my counselor. I can only teach as your witness. I pray that I may become more continually aware that you are always by my side.

On Sensing the Call to Pray

There are times I just want to pray. Maybe I am at a church service, and I want to pray with the congregation. When I am walking through the neighborhood, I am often touched by the creation surrounding me. The birds, the flowers, green lawns and trees will move me to prayers of praise and thanksgiving for the creation of life itself. I want to thank God for all sorts of things large and small. It is part of my relationship with Him.

Yet, there are times I feel called to pray. No, it's not a piercing, penetrating command from on High. It is a movement of the Holy Spirit gently stirring from deep within to bring something into my foremost thoughts. I might be reminded of a person again and again throughout the day. I have learned to pray for that person whenever this happens. It is one of the

Break Ground

ways the Lord will call me to intercessory prayer.

A few years ago, I worked several months as a temporary secretary in a research and development group. Among the scientists was George, a wonderful Jewish man deeply committed to serving Yaweh and living according to his traditions. Needless to say, our theology lay worlds apart. Yet we had been born of the same ancient roots, and I was determined to find common ground. During one of our rare conversations on religion, I looked deeply into his eyes and said, "George, there are many differences between us, and I do not want to argue with you about God. However, there is one thing that I do know beyond a doubt. You know Him, and I know that you know Him." At that point, George simply nodded his head very solemnly. I said, "The only real difference is that I have found my Messiah, and you have not yet found yours." It was a precious moment of mutual understanding.

Several months after I left that job, I found myself thinking about George several times a day. After a few days, I realized that maybe something was happening, and maybe the Lord wanted me to pray for George. When I finally began to pray, I found myself understanding a strong movement of the Holy Spirit, and I realized that I had a job to do. Since I really did not know how to pray, I used my gift of tongues. I would pray for a while in tongues; then I would feel inspired to pray for a while in English. Sometimes I turned to the scriptures and personalized the psalms, asking the Lord to accept my prayer as if they came from George. For over three months, I prayed for this man whenever I thought about him. That was almost every day, several times a day, and sometimes in the middle of the night. One day I realized that I had not prayed for George for almost a week, and I thought the need for prayer must be over. So I praised the Lord and thanked him for taking care of George and for allowing me the grace for intercessory prayer.

While shopping two months later, I happened to meet

Betty, who had worked as George's secretary for almost three years. We stopped to chat, and I had a chance to catch up on the news of that group of scientists. I told her that I particularly wanted to ask about George because I had felt the need to pray for him for about three months. Her mouth dropped open in complete surprise! George had needed many prayers because he had suffered two heart attacks and by-pass surgery during those very same months. He had almost died more than once. Yet he had survived and eventually returned to work with a reduced workload. If he took care of himself, the doctors believed he would live many more years. My prayers had been needed, and I believe the Lord arranged my meeting with Betty so that I could be affirmed in that call to pray. Now it doesn't take me several days or a week to realize what is happening. As soon as I realize that I am thinking repeatedly about someone, I begin to pray as the Lord leads. That may mean one simple little prayer or many. Over a period of time, there have been so many validations of the need for those prayers that I no longer question the call to pray.

On the Quest for Guidance in Prayer

Sensing the call to pray is only the beginning. If we are to respond in obedience to the will of the Lord, then we must also understand how to pray. Of course, the best way to accomplish that is simply to ask the Lord, "How do you want me to pray?" Then stop to pray about that and make yourself open to wherever the Holy Spirit may lead. It is seldom wise for us to pray purely from our own intellectual understanding of the circumstances and the people involved. Only God truly knows the dimensions of the problem and what is in that person's heart. It is, however, always wise to pray for the Lord's will to be done in any set of circumstances and for any person. Often the prayer is sufficient, although sometimes more is needed. You might be asked to

Break Ground

share the pain or grief.

When an acquaintance named Barbara tragically lost her son a few years ago, I was vicariously burdened with her grief for several weeks. This brave Christian lady had also lost her husband just a couple of years before the son's fatal accident. So much grief in such a short period of time must have been overwhelming. However, I knew that I was not alone in sharing her heartache because many people had known and loved this family. Months passed and suddenly I began to awaken occasionally in the middle of the night thinking about Barbara and experiencing an incredible sense of loneliness. This was one time the Lord did not have to nag me or show me repeatedly what to do. He was calling me to pray for Barbara and specifically to intercede for her suffering in loneliness. Sometimes I would pray for only ten minutes or so before I sensed a lifting of the burden within myself. Sometimes the task took hours. Two weeks later, I saw her at church.

"Barbara, I don't know what is going on in your life, nor do I want to ask. I just want you to know that I have been praying a lot for you lately, sometimes in the middle of the night. I'm not looking for any thanks. I'm just trying to say one thing. You may be by yourself at times, but you are never really alone!" She could say nothing as tears filled her eyes, and we both silently gave thanks unto the Lord.

Not all of my "midnight calls" are received so clearly. One night I had awakened and simply could not return to sleep. When the idea of reading the Bible occurred to me, I began to browse through the Psalms with the notion of seeking guidance for prayer. Suddenly my eyes were riveted onto the following scripture:

> I cry aloud to God, aloud to God, that he may
>   hear me.
> In the day of my trouble I seek the Lord;

in the night my hand is stretched out without
wearying; my soul refuses to be comforted.
I think of God, and I moan;
I meditate, and my spirit faints,
Thou dost hold my eyelids from closing
I am so troubled that I cannot speak.

Psalm 77:1-4 (RSV)

As I read these words, I realized that the psalmist was crying out for help and that I was feeling a deep spiritual movement within myself. At that time, there were no terribly overwhelming problems in my life. In other words, I was not particularly worried about anything. So, this call for help must be for someone else. "Who needs help, Lord?"

Then I thought of my friend Neil, who was my teammate in teaching Sunday school. I began to hold him close to the Lord and to pray for him. I prayed the entire Psalm 77 for him over and over. The Holy Spirit drew near and bound himself to Neil and I as a threefold cord, which could not be broken. For me, it was a new dimension of intercessory prayer and a very disturbing experience. I lay in my bed interceding and thinking of Neil for almost two hours before I felt relieved of the urgency to pray and released to return to sleep.

On the following Sunday, I found a moment to share the experience with Neil. He was astonished by my story. The same night I had prayed, Neil had experienced a terrible, sleepless night filled with nightmares of anxiety and confusion. Earlier that day, he had finally made some very important decisions in his life—decisions which were according to the will of God and decisions which required a deeper commitment to Our Lord. When he went to bed, he began to toss and turn in an anguish he could only describe as some sort of spiritual attack, because he arose in the morning with a distinct sense of victory. He felt that he had been to hell and back with Jesus. The battle was over, and it had been won!

As I listened, it was my turn to feel astonished.

On Clearing the Channels

Sometimes we cannot pray according to the Holy Spirit because our channels of communication are clogged with spiritual garbage. I'm talking about problems like bitterness, unforgiveness, hurt feelings, and distress. Unforgiveness abides within a person like a cancer. It prevents joy and love from flowing through people. It is an obstacle to inner peace. It just sits inside putrefying and stinking up the soul like a filthy beast gorging upon each breath of anger. However, it's not always easy to even think about forgiving someone, much less making the decision to do so.

It would be nice if I could say that I never had difficulty in forgiving someone, but this is not so. Over the years I have learned a deep truth as I have suffered through unforgiveness toward release, sometimes repentance, and the ultimate goal of resolution. The barrier is within myself. Either I don't really want to forgive the person, or I cannot forgive him for some reason.

In the first instance, I may not want to forgive the person. At one time in my life, there was a person I'll call Joe, who manipulated and used me to attain his goals. Although he never really told me lies, Joe used half-truths and innuendoes to lead me down the path of his own thinking. He also played upon my feelings by "sharing his pain" and even crying in sorrow over the things he had done to hurt people. Eventually, I realized that in many respects Joe was a superb con artist, who had fooled me with the veneer of a practicing Christian totally committed to following the Lord. I disengaged from the church projects we had been working on together, and I made as much space between us as possible. I was the victim who righteously felt betrayed by her loyal friend. Nor did I want to forgive him. I felt too hurt to even consider it.

God's timing was perfect for our pastor to preach upon the sin of unforgiveness.

> Judge not, and you will not be judged; condemn not, and you will not be condemned; forgive, and you will be forgiven....
> *Luke 6:37 (RSV)*

> Bear with one another and, if anyone has a complaint against another, forgive each other; just as the Lord has forgiven you, so you also must forgive.
> *Col. 3:13 (NRSV)*

I listened, I thought, and I decided to forgive Joe. In a prayer before the altar at church, I told the Lord that I had forgiven Joe, and then I asked the Lord to forgive me for my own bad attitude of unforgiveness. After I spiritually laid these things upon the altar of God, I walked away feeling relieved. I had gotten bogged down in the mire of spiritual decay. Now I was joyfully free to move forward again.

There are times, however, when the basic decision to forgive is simply not enough. The hurt may lie too deep, and the damage might be too devastating. I'm thinking of the survivors of sexual abuse, especially those abused during childhood. Some time ago, I learned that I am one of those victims. I know that I must forgive the perpetrators, and I have committed myself to do so by the grace of God.

> Let all bitterness and wrath and anger and clamor and slander be put away from you, with all malice, and be kind to one another, tenderhearted, forgiving one another, as God in Christ forgave you.
> *Ephesians 4:31-32 (RSV)*

Right now, I have already forgiven with my mind, but my

heart has not been able to follow. I must experience both psychological and spiritual inner healing. It took months just for the trauma of the revelation of abuse to pass. Although I will be in recovery for years, perhaps the rest of my life, it is not my intention to harbor bitterness and anger. I've learned to let the bitterness and anger vomit forth and to keep praying. I give the filth to the Lord and trust him for the disposal. But, sometimes forgiveness is not a one-time event. It reminds me of peeling an onion with never-ending layers to the problem. So, I trust God to heal my wounds and give me the grace I need to completely forgive someday. And, I keep a cross on my bedroom wall to remind me that the Lord died for the sins of the abuser as well as for me.

On Cursing the Evil One

There is a force in this world that opposes the love of God. It is an evil presence called the devil and personified by names like Satan or Beelzebub. The name does not matter; it is evil and it is very real. The Bible refers to demoniacs, that is, people who were possessed by demons. Delivering these poor souls from demons was part and parcel of the ministry of Jesus. He even gave the disciples power to cast out demons.

Some of these "deliverances" might have been medical cures as with the mute in Matthew 9:32, the epileptic boy in Mark 9:17, or the blind and mute demoniac of Matthew 12:22. In biblical times, many illnesses were simply attributed to demons. I do not believe that was always the true explanation. When I look at the man with the unclean spirit in Luke 4:32 and the demoniac at Gadara in Matthew 8:28, I believe these healings were true exorcisms performed by Jesus with the spiritual authority of God.

> They were all amazed and kept saying to one another, "What kind of utterance is this? For with authority and power he commands the unclean

spirits, and out they come!"

Luke 4:36 (NRSV)

Exorcisms are not just an event of the past, they are performed today in various churches by people who have been empowered by the Lord with a special ministry in deliverance. It can be a dangerous procedure, just like surgery. Deliverance from evil spirits should only be performed by well-trained men and women of God acting only upon the guidance and authority of the Holy Spirit. This is not the type of prayer for most people to practice. Do not curse the evil one. Stay away from it. If you believe that someone is possessed by an evil spirit, first pray for spiritual protection for yourself and all others present, and then pray for the Lord to quiet the spirit and to send a deliverer. Mentally hold the victim close to the Lord and pray for divine love and peace to descend on that person. No more.

On Knowing When the Job is Done

Knowing when to pray and how to pray is only part of the job. To pray according to the Holy Spirit means also to understand when to stop praying, in other words, to know when the intercessory job is done, and it's time to praise the Lord and thank him for answered prayer. Sometimes this is easy, particularly when you have feedback from other people that the prayer has been answered. In my life, I most often receive this type of feedback along my prayer chain or in the women's support groups I attend. Sometimes announcements are made at church to thank God for the answer to prayers. Other times, it is just quiet news passed from one prayer partner to another. But what about those times there is no friendly feedback from other people?

How do we know when to stop praying? This requires discernment and guidance from the Holy Spirit. Since each of us has a different relationship to the Lord, it follows that each of us may understand his guidance in a distinct manner. Therefore, I cannot tell you exactly how you will know. In time and with practice in waiting upon the Lord and listening to the Holy Spirit, the communication will come. Eventually you will clearly know when you have been released from the call to pray.

Years ago, my son Daniel was under the care of Dr. Mary Bains, a wonderful and loving physician whom I admired and respected. One day I received news that Dr. Bains had lost her husband of many years. This was at the time I was learning to pray by daily interceding for people on my prayer list. I added her name to my list, and I began to pray for her. Several days later, I felt strongly impelled to call her. After I nervously dialed the telephone, I was surprised to hear her voice because she did not usually answer the phone directly. I found myself feeling a bit startled. I stumbled through an apology for interrupting her, took and deep breath, and blurted out a few words about praying for her at this difficult time of her life. She simply said, "Thank you." Although I felt foolish and even embarrassed by my remarks, I also knew that I had acted out of an attitude of obedience to what I believe the Lord was telling me to do.

Less than a month later, I noticed that whenever I began to pray for Dr. Bains, I felt a stirring of lightness within myself, a sense of relief or release. Eventually I wondered if I should continue to pray for her, but I had no reason to desist, except for the funny feeling that she no longer needed my prayers. So I continued to pray for her and all of the others on my prayer list because I was still disciplining myself to do so everyday. A couple of months later, I called her office to make an appointment for Daniel. The answering service informed me the office was closed and gave me another doctor's number to call. When I reached the receptionist, I was sadly informed that Dr. Bains had died just about the time I had started to question my need to continue those prayers. Because I had not recognized that the Lord was guiding me, I had continued to pray for over two months after her death!

It took several experiences over a long period of time for the Lord to teach me how to understand when to stop praying. The Lord is very patient and loving with his children.

For a time I tried to "track" my prayer results whenever I began to sense the need to pray diminishing inside of me. I soon learned that sometimes I could validate my feelings and sometimes not. It became a matter of my trusting the Lord to get the message through to me. Eventually I quit attempting to confirm the need to cease prayer. I've learned that the continual quest for guidance is a lifetime affair. Not coincidentally, I seem to receive just enough information from amazing sources to affirm my direction whenever I need it. It's primarily an effort on my part just to keep my spiritual antenna up and listening. Then if I am willing to follow, the Lord is always willing to lead.

In Summary, the ultimate goal of the Christian is to pray according to the Holy Spirit. Since this means praying beyond human understanding, it becomes part and parcel of our relationship with God. We are always free to love Him through prayers of praise and thanksgiving and to approach Him with supplication and petitions. As our intimacy grows, we no longer have to think about "what to pray", but we reach to Him spontaneously—running into His arms.

Remember that all prayer, to be effective, must conform to the word of God, the Bible. That is, prayer must never conflict with scripture, the precepts and commandments of the Lord. Then as one matures in prayer life, he or she learns to understand or "sense" the call to pray. Pay attention to your thoughts, because it may be God calling upon you to stand in the gap with intercessory prayer. It could be an unexplainable moment of knowledge or a sudden conviction that you need to pray. It could be persistent nagging thoughts of a person or a set of circumstances. Pay attention and take action.

When called to pray, remember to ask the Lord how to pray. He will guide and direct your paths to accomplish His purpose through the Holy Spirit. This is a time to grow in prayer and in trusting the Lord. Your primary job is to listen and to obey until released from the task. Father will make sure you learn His signals.

Questions for Discussion:

1. Have you ever felt spiritually called to pray, and how did you understand that summons?

2. The keys to understanding are to spiritually pay attention, listen, and learn to be guided by the Holy Spirit. It is mostly a matter of your availability to God. Read John 16:13.

3. Understanding the summons is the first step. The second step is asking the Lord how to pray. Read I John 5:14. Remember that your prayers need not be confined to words.

4. If you have obstacles to your prayer (bitterness or unforgiveness), give those horrible feelings to Jesus. Picture a symbol of the problem alongside an onion, and ask the Lord to peel off another layer. Reference Hebrews 7:25 and 10:22-23.

5. Leave the demons to those with a proven ministry of exorcism. Simply protect yourself and others by putting on the full armor of God by personalizing Eph. 6:14-18 as a prayer.

6. Wait upon the Lord to learn when to stop praying. If you ask him for clear guidance, he will give it to you. Look at Psalm 33:20 and Hebrews 3:14.

CHAPTER ELEVEN

On Prayer as a Way of Life

Thank you, Lord, for walking hand in hand with me through the writing of this book. Please help me to assimilate what has been written so that the lessons to be learned may be completed according to your will. Thank you.

When I began to write *Break Ground,* I did an analysis on all the types of prayer and methods of prayer I had ever experienced or witnessed in my Christian walk. I have tried to share them with you in hope that you may discover a new path to tread or a more comfortable way to pray. When I pray, however, I seldom stop to analyze or decide upon a process or method of prayer to use at any given moment. If I pray according to the Holy Spirit, then I am praying in accordance with the guidance and direction of the Lord. For me, this usually means all sorts of combinations and methods of prayer. It's an assimilation of all that I have written and experienced. The prayer flows forth spontaneously like talking, walking, and breathing. I don't think very much on how I am praying, I just do it.

Very little of my total prayer time is spent on my knees or

in church, or even in a quiet reverent position anywhere. I pray here at my computer because the words don't flow quickly. Composition is a burden and a chore to me and has been so all my life. Yet, the Lord has called me to write contemplations, prayers, and teachings. By his grace I am writing—certainly not by my own human accomplishment. Where I am most weak, I can only become strong through Christ, who strengthens me. At the same time I feel both humbled and very grateful.

The Lord is gracious to hear my prayers anywhere, in the shower, at work, in play, and in my rest. We have spent much of my driving time together and days of planting and weeding the garden. We often chat while I am washing dishes, doing laundry, or shopping. His presence is always with me, just like my body is always with my mind. We cannot be separate, but that does not mean that I always think about God, just as I do not always think about my body or my mind. There is simply unity in being, constant accessibility, unrelenting presence. I listen to my dreams, pay attention to my visions, and pray for understanding as well as guidance. Prayer has become a way of life through which my gift of faith is nurtured and strengthened. Without the knowledge of God and his spiritual gifts, I do not believe I could have survived or healed from the sorrows of my life.

On a Season of Grief

The events surrounding my father's death and the subsequent period of grief was a season of prayer and sustenance by faith. When I returned home, I wrote the following open letter to the congregation of my church and published it as an article in the monthly newsletter.

I Heard Your Prayers

Thank you for loving me and praying for me and

On Prayer as a Way of Life

my family during our crisis. On August 23 my mother was hospitalized with her multiple health problems seriously complicated by the onset of diabetes. She weighed only 76 pounds, a living scarecrow. One week later my father collapsed with congestive failure, and I rushed down south to Mississippi. We endured a month-long nightmare caring for both parents, moving our mother to a nursing home, and watching our father battle death, victorious on several occasions until that final night of hemorrhaging.

Through it all I felt your prayers; I heard them in the Holy Spirit whenever I paused to look to the Lord; and I saw the prayer results constantly in the circumstances surrounding me. All of my needs were met from quickly finding parking space on each hospital visit to that final departure at 5:00 A.M. As I stumbled through my tears out of the elevator with my arms overloaded with Daddy's things, there was an angel crossing my path. A young man in hospital garb (complete with stethoscope) stopped to carry my packages and to escort me to my car in the still dark parking lot. He was gently compassionate as he cautioned me to lock up and to be very careful driving home. He waited until my crying subsided before saying good-bye. And, I knew that God had sent him. It was no coincidence; it was the action of amazing grace leveraged by your prayer power.

I never felt alone because the Lord was always with me as well as the hearts of all of you who cared enough to pray. Thank you for being there. I am truly blessed!

             Margaret

During the events described in my letter, I really spent little time actively praying. I asked the Lord for intercessors and trusted him to meet my needs. My hours were too busy and stress-filled for me to focus on prayer. For a short while, I even lost the ability to concentrate sufficiently for safe driving, which was proved the night I drove through a red light at a very dangerous intersection. Thank the Lord, there was a policeman driving right behind me; and he gave me a ticket. The incident forced me to understand that my level of functioning was at ebb tide. I reassessed my condition and sought medical help and increased rest, a difficult accomplishment under the circumstances.

There was one night that I simply prayed for the ability to pray and received an answer in the Lord's peace, which passes understanding. That was the night my father died.

I was temporarily alone in the waiting room outside of the intensive care unit. In my lap lay the Amplified Bible I had borrowed from my niece. With a brief prayer for guidance, I opened the Bible and began to browse through scripture. I believe I received insight from the following bits and pieces of scripture:

Chapter 12 of Joshua.

When David's time to die was near, he charged Solomon his son, saying, I go the way of all the earth.

I Kings 2:1-2

...and you shall know with an acquaintance and understanding based on and grounded in personal experience that I am the Lord: for they shall not be put to shame who wait for, look for, hope for and expect Me.

Isaiah 49:23

Chapter 12 of the Book of Joshua is composed of 24 verses listing the kings of the lands whom the Israelites defeated. It is a message of victory over many battles. It spoke to me of my father's battles in lifetime, and it gave me hope for his spiritual victory over death. The verse from I Kings simply affirmed to me that my father was going to die that night.

The second verse puzzled me a little bit. Did it speak to my relationship to God or to my father's relationship to God? I knew two things: (1) My father had lived outside of the church for most of my life, and (2) he did not remember the priest giving him absolution along with the last rites of Holy Unction earlier in his hospitalization. As I was thinking upon these things, Father Jim (the priest) walked down the hall towards the intensive care unit. I ran out to tell him that my father did not remember his blessing because I knew that Father Jim needed to understand this before visiting Daddy for the last time. Again, God's timing was perfect.

The priest ministered reconciliation with the Lord to my father, blessed him, and prayed the last rites over him. Then much of the physical and emotional agony left my father, enabling him to calm down and to stop fighting his restraints. Father Jim reported that he appeared significantly more peaceful after the prayers. Twenty minutes later, Daddy was put on the ventilator to mechanically breathe for him, and he received medication putting him to sleep. My father never knew consciousness again. His was a Calvary salvation, like the thief on the cross next to Jesus.

On Amazing Grace

As perceived through the eyes of faith, the events of my father's passage were not coincidental. Every circumstance derived from amazing grace. The Lord was there all of the time during my father's suffering and the tribulations of our family. For a while I wondered why there was so much pain and agony. Why couldn't my father simply die and finally be at peace. Upon reflection, the only reason that I could understand was that Daddy's soul was not yet ready for death. I knew that Our Lord takes no pleasure in our sufferings. Yet, Jesus waited patiently with tears in his own eyes until my father was reconciled unto him. Then Daddy was released from his bondage here on earth to be joyfully received in heaven.

As I continue through the years of my life, I am learning to drop the concept of coincidence out of my life. Whenever things seem to weave nicely together, I begin to recognize amazing grace in action. Through the eyes of faith, I can understand these "coincidences" as the Lord's hand upon my life in even the most small and intimate details. It is one of the ways that I can practice the presence of God. I simply give praise to the Lord and thank him for orchestrating my life.

On Receiving a Message

At a gathering in the Green Mountains of Vermont, my friend Les mentioned that he had written a couple of chapters on a book about harvesting the fruits of the spirit. Chatting about his plans brought to my mind thoughts of my own abandoned book on prayer begun years ago. I wondered at the time if these were just thoughts related to our conversation, or if this might be a nudge from the Lord to complete the project. By now, I had learned that if Father wanted me to do something, He would continue to speak to me in various ways until I either got the message or became very determined to ignore it!

The following week at church, upon first sight of Vicki, our new editor of the monthly newsletter, the word story jumped into my thoughts. I said nothing. When I passed by her in the halls after church, again the word story came to the forefront of my mind. Twenty minutes later, in the parish hall she came to me complaining about insufficient material for the newsletter, and she specifically requested me to write an article to help her. At that point I confessed the "story" nudge and agreed to dig out my old incomplete manuscript to find an appropriate excerpt to submit.

I have no doubt that the Lord orchestrated these events, especially because Vicki became excited when she discovered I had the basic outline of a complete book. She effusively encouraged me to continue writing by affirming my composition skills and responding enthusiastically to the outline. Until then I had never had such concrete support on the project. It was wonderful! However, I warned her about getting too excited. It is much more important to understand the peace of the Lord in these matters, and to know that it is his will. I needed to put emotions aside and depend upon his grace to accomplish anything.

Nevertheless, I believe He placed Vicki in my life as the little angel at my side to help show me the way. I briefly prayed for additional confirmation that the Lord wanted me to complete this book. It's the same old story with me. I have to ask the Lord to make me understand his message clearly, or I will probably just generate great problems solving the ills of the world my way.

"Lord, please spiritually hit my over the head if you want me to do this, so that I may get the message very clearly. Thank you."

That night I had a dream in four parts.

<u>Scene One</u>: The doctor informed me that I was pregnant with triplets. This was a surprise because I didn't feel pregnant. However, I couldn't refute the sight of my enlarged belly when I looked down. So, I asked when he thought I might be due to deliver. He said, "Maybe four to six weeks." I wondered if I might have to be hospitalized during the final weeks. He said that would not be necessary as I was "doing fine" and he anticipated no real problems. He did want to monitor me closely, and he wanted to send me to have a test

to make sure all of the babies' heartbeats were healthy. Otherwise, no extra tests or medical treatments. As I left his office, I looked again at my belly and thought that I just didn't look very big for a person so far along with triplets. It was all so very difficult for me to believe. Maybe the next few weeks would make a tremendous difference, and I would blow up magnificently!

<u>Scene Two</u>: Then I walked down the street, wandering into a nearby church to pray. I saw my friend Claudia sitting in church. She was pregnant, too! She looked about midway through gestation. I was about to go over to talk to her when I passed by Rose Kennedy sitting in a pew and reading a book. Her book was opened up to the inspirational story of how her son Jack Kennedy and his crew survived the sinking of his PT-109 boat in World War II.

<u>Scene Three</u>: My sneakers and socks were sitting under my desk.

<u>Scene Four</u>: I saw a typewritten page and a couple of empty bottles that had been rinsed out in preparation for recycling.

I understood the dream as further communication from the Lord leading me to return to the project of writing this book. In the first scene, I am very pregnant, that is, filled with life. The number three symbolizes the complete Godhead to me; and I therefore understand the three babies to symbolize the complete spiritual growth of this composition. Birthing, or writing the book, is imminent and might not take long, if I disciplined myself and paid attention to gifts of creativity and inspiration. Since there is no need for early hospitalization, extra testing or procedures, I am not to be anxious as there should be no difficult problems to remedy. The close monitoring indicates the Lord will keep his hand upon the very pulse of my work. Meanwhile, I am just having a little trouble understanding that I really do have a book inside of me and the test will confirm the healthy heartbeats of that literary life.

The second scene tells me to commit an act of faith as I am walking into the church to commune with God over these strange tidings. Seeing my friend Claudia appearing five or six months pregnant brings two thoughts to my understanding. First of all, she is much too old to bear children, so this must be a miracle child! Secondly, I admire Claudia as a professional businesswoman, and I want to connect her condition symbolically with the birthing of new business. The presence of Rose Kennedy is also noteworthy as a woman who has birthed many babies, including an important president of the United States. The page opened to the PT-109 story speaks of inspirational literature. Perhaps someone, somewhere, will be able to find inspiration in these musings. Only God knows, and my dears, IT IS HIS BUSINESS—not yours and not mine.

Scene three depicts my walking shoes and tells me very clearly to quit walking away from the chore, sit down at my desk, and get going.

Scene four is specific guidance and instruction to start by recycling the old typewritten chapters written long ago. This was actually first accomplished by the article I had given to Vicki for the church newsletter.

Six days after the dream, I finally reviewed my work for edit, and I began to write again. Thank God for his patience with me. I am not the fastest on the draw in the obedience department. As I now approach my final words here, I look back upon a season of spiritual groaning (Romans 8:22) and travail to achieve the birth of this book. As in all acts of creation, the work was begun and ended by the Holy Spirit. It was an honor to be along for the ride.

In Summary, prayer easily become a lifestyle as a person draws closer to the Lord. Prayer as a way of life means practicing the presence of God as a lifelong habit beginning with the simple commitment to pray. This leads to an increased desire to know Him personally, as well as through scripture.

During difficult times, it is often impossible to pray—for ourselves, or anyone else needing prayer. Admit your need for help, lean on the Lord, and allow the Holy Spirit to guide you. Cry to the Lord for help, and do not hesitate to ask for intercessors! Our Lord loves to call upon his children to pray for one another.

It is important to spiritually listen and to learn the difference between coincidence and amazing grace. Ask God to teach you to view all of the circumstances of your life through the eyes of faith. If you should feel incompetent to understand the answers to your prayer, do not hesitate to ask the Lord to make his message very, very clear. Just put your spiritual antenna on reception mode and expect an answer.

Finally, you and I have broken ground on learning how to pray. We have defined prayer as communication, commitment, and relationship with the Lord, who always answers our prayer. We have reviewed the various types of prayer, both individual and corporate (with others); and we have explored new methods. Effective prayer can be formal or informal, liturgical or non-liturgical. Songs of worship and spirit-filled dance are also powerful ways to pray, as well as a simple conversation with God.

Since communication with God is a two-way experience, we have learned how to listen—how to hear from the Lord! First and foremost, He speaks to us through the Bible. He also speaks to us through the circumstances and events of our lives, as well as through other people. Our thought lives are another highway for communication. We must pay attention to our thoughts, for they may contain the voice of the Lord. Sometimes take a little browse through the Bible to see if a verse sort of "leaps out" to you. Give the Lord your attention.

Praise the Lord! We have moved beyond the boundaries

of words to express the joy and gratitude of divine love. The use of mental images to project our prayers can be more powerful than any attempt to vocalize our thoughts. Dreams and visions from the Lord are just as real today as they were during Biblical times and must be prayerfully received. We are called to service and sacrifice as a form of prayer. Vicarious suffering is another means of prayer, which the Holy Spirit often uses to summon us. And of course, we recognize the Lord's peace beyond understanding as powerful communion with Him.

Because He is truth, God is both mystical and mysterious—far beyond our comprehension. Heaven-sent dreams, vision, and words of knowledge herald the walk of Christian mysticism. Further, we can encounter God's mysticism through prayerful meditations, contemplation, and journalizing the Word. We have examined the laying on of hands and prayer for healing, and we have investigated glossolalia, that is the gift of tongues—a prayer language from the Holy Spirit.

Although we have explored all of these avenues of prayer, it is of no consequence until we have learned to pray according to the Holy Spirit. What we might think to pray may not be what is needed. Only the Lord knows. The most effective prayer, therefore, is that for which we have been summoned and have received guidance. It is important that we not allow our spiritual radar to become fouled with anger, hurt, and bitterness. Place these things upon the altar of repentance that God may cleanse and heal you. Then you may proceed forward to complete the job for which you have been called.

As you continue to explore the many avenues of prayer, you may find that prayer becomes a lifestyle of intimacy with the Lord. He will bless you with the knowledge of His presence through grief, as well as joy. You will find His grace in action through your prayers and receive blessings without end.

On My Prayer for You

> Lord, I thank you for sharing this book with my sisters and brothers in Christ. Use the meditations of my heart and the works of my hands as an instrument of peace in their lives. Please bless them and teach them to pray so that they might draw nearer unto you. May they learn to seek your face and to experience the knowledge of God that leads into the deeper spiritual waters of commitment, relationship and understanding. Let the obstacles be crushed and the mountains fall that would impede their progress onto the path of your light and your holiness. I pray that they would come to know you more fully and to better understand the leading of the Holy Spirit. Let us proclaim that all good things come from you, O Lord, and to you be all of the honor and the glory. Amen

Questions for Discussion:

1. How, when and where do you pray? Write your answers on a separate sheet of paper to be saved in your Bible, and answer the same questions again next year, and the next year. Watch how you have grown.

2. Look at I Samuel 7:8 and 12:19 for Old Testament examples of intercession. Read Ephesians 1:16-19 and Collosians 1:9 for New Testament examples. Share an experience of intercession.

3. Can you share an event in your life that could be either labeled as luck, or understood to be an answer to prayer?

4. Read John 10:3-4. Discuss some of your problems on

"hearing from the Lord."

5. End the session with prayers of praise and thanksgiving, and give God the glory for what you have learned. Amen.

Break Ground Ministries, Inc.

Dave and Margaret Calkin are missionaries commissioned by Fields of Harvest Ministries, International with a joint ministry of prayer and helps. They founded Break Ground Ministries, Inc., bringing formal structure to the work they have been doing for years helping small churches and startup ministries.

A natural evolution of publishing Break Ground on Learning How to Pray is a new prayer ministry accessible through our web site at www.BreakGroundMinistries.com. Visit us there to find more information about us and discover how we may help you through prayer and helps. Perhaps you may wish to help us, too. Pray about it!

All donations, royalties, or profits derived from the sale of this book will be paid directly to Break Ground Ministries, Inc.